COOKING
TO THE GLORY OF GOD

Calvin M. Howell

A Collection of Vegan Recipes

"And God said, Behold, I have given you every herb bearing seed...
and every tree in the which is the tree yielding fruit..."
Genesis 1:29

Published by:
CALVIN M. HOWELL
480 Neely Lane, Huntingdon, TN 38344 • calvinmhowell@yahoo.com

ACKNOWLEDGEMENTS

DEDICATION

To my wife, who always encourages me to press forward against all discouragements and to continue aided by heavenly agencies to formulate recipes that will be a blessing to many.

ACKNOWLEDGEMENTS

I want to thank everyone who contributed their recipes, suggestions, and prayers. Also, for those who enlisted their influences in promoting this humble book to their families, friends, and at meetings.

I am truly grateful to Odis Anthony, the cover designer; Monik Amelia for formatting skills/Editor; Joan Sartin who created the title; the health guest that I met eight years ago at M.E.E.T. Ministry for the words that propelled me to move forward against all discouragements, and inadequacies; and for M.E.E.T. Ministry for permitting me to develop as a vegetarian cook, and an author of Cooking to the Glory of God. Finally, I want thank God for the talent He gave for the blessing of someone.

COVER DESIGNER	Odis Anthony
BOOK FORMATTER	Monik Amelia
RESEARCHER	Calvin Howell

TABLE OF CONTENTS

Denotes – Cookbook Recipes

I was born and raised in Cleveland, Ohio with seven other siblings. Before I reached the double digits, I was cooking grits, eggs, and bacon. In my teens, I had advanced to spaghetti, chitterlings, chicken, and etc. In short, in my early years it was normal to find me in the kitchen. And, might I add, I did learn a few things from my step-father who also was a cook, and who cooked most of time. But, in all this, cooking was not even among the top 10 list of what I wanted to do in life.

In July of 1994, I enlisted into USMC, and it was in a boot camp that I began to develop a desire for God separate from other influences. The intensity of boot camp made Sunday services the place to be on Sunday morning for a period of relief. After graduating from boot camp, I was sent to Camp Geiger in North Carolina for Marine Combat Training. It was here that the Lord began to prepare me for my future work. At that time I was not a Christian, and therefore did not recognize God's providential hand working in my life. One day, before finishing my time there, the corporal came into the barracks with some forms in his hands. He called for everyone's attention, and upon obtaining it he proceeded to inform us of our MOS. When he came to me he said "Howell, you're a cook". I was rather surprised, and in my mind, I looked at cooking as being inferior to all other MOS's. Nevertheless, I was impressed to just accept the outcome, besides it might not be that bad after all, I thought. I would take cooking anytime of the day than to be a grunt. And this was great since I loved to eat, and fast at that. Off to Camp Johnson I went, where I began my training as a cook.

A year later, I was discharged from the military due to physical challenges. I remember the day that things took a turn for me in the military. By this time I really did not like the Marine Corp anymore. I was essentially done with all of my training. One day, I went to sick bay due to back pains. The medical personnel asked did I have back pains prior to enlisting. I replied, "Yes". He styled it, "erroneous enlistment", and ask me a question that was surprising, "Do you want to get out?" Immediately, I said, yes! I was then put on a medical board, and was eventually honorably discharged in a couple of months.

The following year was a very eventful, stressful, and depressing year. In my heart, I was developing a desire for change in my life. I remember praying to God saying, "God bring me into your church before You come". Of course, I did not fully understand what I was asking, nor did I recognize God's providential leading in my life. A year later, I was invited after so many times to come to church. I eventually came, and I never stopped going. When I thought to leave, a voice said to me, "If you go, you will not change". So, I decided to stay. During this time I was working at the Hometown Buffet, formerly called "Old Country Buffet" as a dishwasher, until my boss, impressed with my work ethics, asked me to become a cook. I accepted, but it still wasn't my desire.

I had read a book entitled "Counsels on Diets and Foods" and was convinced that I should leave off certain articles of food. I eventually stopped working at the Hometown Buffet because of my conviction in regards to cooking unclean and harmful foods.

In 1998, I was introduced to a ministry called M.E.E.T. Ministry by my sister Natalie. My sister had had an experience here and thought she would share the blessings she encountered. I was asked by the assistant director to come down as a volunteer for three weeks, and I consented to come. The three weeks turned into nine months; an opportunity to go through their, then, three-month training school (now it is four months), and an opportunity to begin my quest as a vegetarian cook. I would occasionally help out in the kitchen with Sister Gentles who was the main cook. Upon graduating from school, there was an opening for me to go to Bengin, Washington to take someone's place for four months as a cook at Mother's Market. I remember praying to God to help me learn all I could in one week. My prayer was answered! It was here that I had an opportunity to cook, thus developing my skills as a vegetarian cook.

In 2001, I was hired as hygienic therapist at M.E.E.T. Ministry. I did not want to become a cook. I felt I didn't need any help in this area but, God saw otherwise. Sister Gentles (now Caldwell), the cook, had hurt her knee and couldn't continue working as the cook. Another training school was about to start, so the search began for another cook. Time was winding down, and still no one. As I viewed the situation, I decided to volunteer to help out if no cook could be found. What did I do that for? No sooner did I make that statement, did I become the next cook at the ministry. I really didn't want to do it because I felt so inadequate. But M.E.E.T. Ministry's kitchen became my training ground. Both in cooking skills and in character development!

I continued to grow rather rapidly as a cook. Many would say to me that I should make my own cookbook. Looking at my inadequacies, I would shy away from it. This I did until a health guest came to a health session held at the ministry. She was blessed by my cooking. She said what many had said before, "You should make your own cookbook". I then expressed my inadequacies, until she said something that triggered hope. She said, "You will bless somebody with your cookbook". This was all I needed, and the good Lord had bid me go forward. I started with eight recipes and continued to build upon those eight to where I am today with roughly 160 recipes. Praise God!

On August 29, 2006 I was blessed with the opportunity to conduct a cooking class on the 3ABN Today Show. The show was seen by many and the responses were excellent. On December 27, 2006 I had an opportunity to appear in the Jackson Sun Newspaper with a display of some of the dishes from my cookbook.

In 2004 I moved to Chicago, Illinois to assist Gladys Brown at The Back to Eden Health Center in South Holland, Illinois. There, I had the privilege of conducting a total of 7 cooking schools. This was a blessed and growing experience.

I would like to thank those individuals who were instrumental in helping me accomplish one of my goals in putting together my second cookbook. I am truly thankful for its name, which was chosen by a co-worker at M.E.E.T. Ministry. This name will direct not only me but, many to the word of God as they realize that even cooking should be done to the Glory of God. Cooking has an important place in this world and in the Christians life. Education upon the subject of healthy cooking is of vital importance and is necessary for us if we would present ourselves a living sacrifice.

In producing this book, it is my desire to provide families with recipes and educational information on the subject of health. This will help them to make an intelligent transition from the Standard American Diet (S. A. D.) to Gods Life Activating Diet (G. L. A. D.). Thank you for your support and interest.

Cooking to the Glory of God is one cookbook among many wonderful cookbooks within Seventh-Day Adventism, all are doing their appointed work. I'm thankful for the opportunity to be among many in helping others learn how to eat better, live better, feel better, and be better.

Calvin M. Howell

God created man in His own image, and put him in the land of Eden. Eden had a multi-purpose; it was to be Adam's home, school, place of worship, and of employment. This school was of such a character so as to facilitate or foster character building. Thus, man would become more and more like His Maker. One of the classes would focus on man's diet. In Genesis Chapter 1:29 God taught what is called an "Introductory Class on Man's diet". Though man was perfect he was not "omniscient" meaning "all knowing". He who created man knew what man needed to sustain him physically. God also created beast, fowl, and etc... and the same chose their diet. Man could give a name with much meaning to man as well as to the lower creatures in harmony with the mind of his Maker, but could not choose his own diet, subsequently the diet of any lower creature. This inability was not the result of any defect in man, but rather a natural inability known to "ALL CREATED" or "CREATURES". They had the ability to know, but not all things.

In the first nutrition class, God clearly outlined man's diet. God began and ended his class with these authoritative words "Behold, I have given you every herb bearing seed, which [is] upon the face of all the earth, and every tree, in the which [is] the fruit of a tree yielding seed; *to you it shall be for meat.*"[1] (See table 1)   This was a law, and any omission or addition to this diet would either be a violation of the rule, or an exception explicitly granted by "THE CREATOR" Himself!

Let us identify these foods in their respective categories.

Table 1		
The Original Diet		
Herb Yielding Seed (Genesis 1:11)	**Fruit Tree** (Genesis 1:11)	**Herbs of the Field** (Genesis 3:18)
Grains	Fruits	Vegetables
Nuts		Legumes
Seeds		Tubers

Vegetables were an addition to the original diet. This addition was not a violation, but a permanent addition given by God. In addition to this change there were two other changes in the Original Diet. One was an omission, the other an addition, one authorized by God, and the other was prohibited by God.

THE "PROHIBITION"

At creation God explicitly instructed Adam concerning the foods that were permitted to eat, and the foods that were prohibited. In Genesis, God gave Adam His commandment saying, "Of every tree of the garden thou mayest freely eat: But of the tree of the knowledge of good and evil, thou shalt not eat of it: for in the day that thou eatest thereof thou shalt surely die."[2] This commandment was clear. The tree of the knowledge of good and evil was the only prohibition given man. This tree was created on the third day of creation, and was declared to be good. Therefore, we can conclude that the tree in and of itself was good, but the result of eating from the "prohibited tree" would be "a knowledge of evil". In other words, to transgress God's definitive commandment merited "only" death, and not life. Since then, the wages of sin has always been death. What is sin? Said John, "Whosoever committeth sin transgresseth also the law: *for sin is the transgression of the law*"[3] currently known as, "the law of God", or the "Ten Commandments". Every one of these commandments is clear, definite, and still binding.

As we behold the creation account we see with undimmed eyes that what we eat can affect our salvation. On the other hand, we are not saved by what we eat. Paul says, *"for by grace are ye saved through faith; and that not of yourselves: it is the gift of God: Not of works, lest any man should boast."*[4] Righteousness does not come by what we eat and drink. It comes by faith! The tree of life did not give righteousness, or life, it only perpetuated the life "that originated from God". If Adam and Eve had been given free access to the tree of life after sin, they would have been immortal sinners, not saints. Says Paul, "Even *the righteousness of God which is by faith of Jesus Christ* unto all and upon all them that believe: for there is no difference"[5]. However, "faith without works is dead".[6] Once we have been recreated or become new creatures, He gives us instructions on health. This He did with Holy Adam after He created Him and with His Holy People "Israel" after He created them.[7] Thus it is, that in the end of time, God wants to give His people instructions on health in a time when disease abound.

God gave Israel health instructions. If He, in His infinite wisdom, sees fit to make any changes in those instructions, we are told exactly how this is would be done. Says Amos, "Surely the Lord GOD will do nothing, but he revealeth his secret unto his servants the prophets"[8]. In Revelation, John predicts that in the end of time, God's last day church would be identified by two distinctive characteristics, "the keeping of the commandments", and "the testimony of Jesus"[9]. The testimony of Jesus is the spirit of prophecy[10]. So, in the end of time, God's last day church would have the special presence of His spirit manifested through the gift of prophecy. Health instructions in the context of the Gospel and Holy Living would come through this channel as it came to Israel by a prophet in the context of being a Holy people. As a result of Adam and Eve violating God's Commandment, they were forbidden free access to the tree of life.

ONE "OMISSION" FROM MAN'S ORIGINAL DIET

Previously we dealt with the diet that was ordained for mankind, by his Maker. That Diet was initially divided into two categories, and eventually into three after the fall of man. We also dealt with the prohibition. Today we will deal with the "omission" from man's diet, "The Tree of Life". It is believed that this was a fruit tree, this being implied by God's command, "Let the earth bring forth grass, the herb yielding seed, *and the fruit tree yielding fruit after his kind*, whose seed is in itself, upon the earth: and it was so."[11] At any rate, this fruit possessed supernatural properties unlike any other food made by God. God said, "Behold, the man is become as one of us, to know good and evil: and now, lest he put forth his hand, and *take also of the tree of life, and eat, and live for ever*... So he drove out the man; and he placed at the east of the garden of Eden Cherubims, and a flaming sword which turned every way, *to keep the way of the tree of life.*"[12] This fruit is no longer a part of man's diet, and therefore the inevitable result is "death". God said to the representative of the human race, "In the sweat of thy face shalt thou eat bread, *till thou return unto the ground; for out of it wast thou taken: for dust thou art, and unto dust shalt thou return.*"[13] This text points to the utter extinction of human life. Will man ever have an opportunity to partake of this tree again? Indeed yes!!! Says John, "Blessed [are] they that do his commandments, that they may have right to the *"tree of life,"* and may enter in through the gates into the city."[14] Those who are obedient will, if they die in Christ be Resurrected from the dead, and given immortality. Say's Paul "For the Lord himself shall descend from heaven with a shout, with the voice of the archangel, and with the trump of God: and the dead in Christ shall rise first"[15] Also, Paul says, "Behold, I show you a mystery; We shall not all sleep, but we shall all be changed, In a moment, in the twinkling of an eye, at the last trump: for the trumpet shall sound, and the dead shall be raised incorruptible, and we shall be changed. For this corruptible must put on incorruption, and this mortal [must] put on immortality. So when this corruptible shall have put on incorruption, and this mortal shall have put on immortality, then shall be brought to pass the saying that is written, Death is swallowed up in victory."[16] What a promise to chew on! Concerning the rest of man's original diet, what are the basic nutrients highlighted in man's diet?

THE BASIC NUTRIENTS IN MAN'S DIET HIGHLIGHTED

The Chart (See table 2) below shows us the Original Diet broken down into essentially three categories.

Table 2		
The Original Diet		
Herb Yielding Seed (Genesis 1:11)	**Fruit Tree** (Genesis 1:11)	**Herbs of the Field** (Genesis 3:18)
Grains	Fruits	Vegetables
Nuts		Legumes
Seeds		Tubers

Why do we eat? "Biologically speaking, people eat to receive nourishment... To maintain your "self" you must continually replenish, from foods, the energy and the nutrients you deplete in maintaining your body."[17] Man's Diet as a whole contains nutrients that yield energy or nutrients that assist energy yielding nutrients. Observe the chart below.

Nutrients	
Energy Yielding Nutrients/Macro-nutrients	Energy Assistant Nutrients/Micro-nutrients
Carbohydrates	Vitamins
Fats	Minerals
Protein	Water

Our loving Creator designed that man shall receive these nutrients from foods. While foods do contain water, man was also to drink water in a concentrated form free from sugar, fiber, pigments, proteins, and vitamins. It is interesting to note that of all the nutrients, only water was to be consumed in a free form. I wonder why! Well, we discuss this in the next section.

THE ROLE OF WATER IN MAN'S DIET

Water is unequivocally the most abundant nutrient in this chart. That there was water at creation is evident from the historical account of Creation given by Moses, "And the earth was without form, and void; and darkness was upon the face of the deep. *And the Spirit of God moved upon the face of the waters...* And God said, Let the *waters under the heaven be gathered together unto one place*, and let the dry land appears: and it was so. And God called the dry land Earth; *and the gathering together of the waters called he Seas*: and God saw that it was good."[18] The waters were declared to be good. Good for what? "And a river went out of Eden to *water the garden*; and from thence it was parted, and became into four heads."[19] These four heads are the beginning of four distinct rivers. At any rate, the water was for the watering of the Garden, subsequently for the growth of all plant life especially those that produce foods. One may argue that before creation the bible does not state explicitly whether or not water in its free form was to be consumed by man. This is true. It is clear however, that water in the foods were essential to man's physical existence, it being a chief component in the foods that God created for man. At the present we obtain roughly 2/3 of our water intake from foods. Water was an essential pleasure before sin. As far as the biblical record is concern, water in its free state was drink for beast and man. "Water has always been an important and life-sustaining drink to humans and is essential to the survival of all organisms."[20]

At the present, water composes 70% or more of man's body. The percentage is higher according to some researchers, and it has been stated by some that the older we get, the less our body's water percentage. At any rate, it can readily be seen that about ¾ of man's body, earth, and food is water. Fruits and vegetables contain 75%-nearly 100% water, and cooked grains contain 60%-69%. Breads would however be about 30%-40% water.

After sin we have much evidence in the bible, and in our daily lives that water in its free form is highly necessary. I refer you to the bible God said, "*In the sweat of thy face* shalt thou eat bread, till thou return unto the ground; for out of it wast thou taken: for dust thou art, and unto dust shalt thou return."[21] We find for the first time the introduction of the word "sweat". What is it that creates sweat? Essentially, sweating (also called perspiring) is the primary way that the body cools itself to maintain a healthy, "normal" temperature. The sweat that appears on the surface of the skin evaporates, causing the cooling that the body needs to maintain a normal temperature.

What causes the body's temperature to increase? "... When the body temperature rises due to physical exercise or a stressful situation, for example, we perspire more. If the surrounding air temperature is higher than is comfortable for the body, we will also perspire more. The body is naturally trying to cool itself."[22] Man who once was naked before sin, now (after sin) needs to be properly clothed to protect him from extreme temperatures. God also made coats of skin and clothed Adam and his wife.[23]

An active person makes the liver more active, and if the liver is active the blood that passes through it becomes heated. The heated blood is then circulated through the whole body. If this continues, the body temperature will exceed normal body temperature, and this will cause the sweat glands to become more active. "Sweat glands under the skin secrete a liquid that is composed of water and small, concentrated amounts of sodium and chloride, which make up the salt compound."[24] It is believed that men's sweat glands are more active than women's sweat glands, as a general rule."[25] Water lost from the lungs and skin accounts for almost one half of the daily losses even when a person is not visibly perspiring; these losses are commonly referred to as insensible water losses"[26] If you remember, God said, *"In the sweat of thy face shalt thou eat bread, till thou return unto the ground"*[27] Bread comes essentially from a grain. Grains are a special kind of seed fruit resulting from a seed that has been planted in a ground that has been tilled or cultivated by man. Man after sin tilled the ground that had been cursed, and that yielded thorns and thistles. Sweat would be accompanied by sorrow all the days of man's life. Adam's first son continued in his fathers steps and became a tiller of the ground.[28]

As we read before, sweat is composed of water and minerals. This loss of water is one of the reasons why water in its free form is needed daily.

How much water does a person need? And what are some of the other benefits of water? Let us answer the former question. Our bodies are composed of systems that are composed of tissues, and tissues that make up cells. Without water cells would die within days. There is no unanimity upon the number of cells in the human body; however the amount of cells in the body can be determined by body size.

Infants, children, and adolescence have fewer body cells than a full grown adult. Infants and etc... are still growing. Their cells are still dividing. This process is called "mitosis". Therefore, your approximate body fluid needs can be determined by following this formula.

Body Weight ÷ 2 = oz. ÷ 8 = cp.	Example: 150lbs. ÷ 2 = 75 oz. ÷ 9.3 cp.

This is actually the minimum. While water is lost through the skin, it is also lost through respiration, urination, and defecation. A diet high in sodium will also increase ones need for water. In order to balance sodium levels, the kidney needs water to excrete excess sodium. Also, a diet that is high in sugar, and highly acidic foods (flesh foods and derivatives) will increase our fluid needs. The kidneys need water in order to balance the sugar levels as well p_H Levels.

"In health and in sickness, pure water is one of heaven's choicest blessings. Its proper use promotes health. It is the beverage, which God provided to quench the thirst of animals and man." "Drunk freely, it helps to supply the necessities of the system and assists nature to resist disease. The external application of water is one of the easiest and most satisfactory ways of regulating the circulation of the blood. A cold or cool bath is an excellent tonic. Warm baths open the pores and thus aid in the elimination of impurities. Both warm and neutral baths soothe the nerves and equalize the circulation."[29] Nehemiah said that God, "gavest them water for their thirst.[30]

Water is the most abundant liquid nutrient, and nutrient in general that we need. A thorough study of the scriptures will inform of us many occasions where water was promised by God, where Jesus thirst, where Israel murmured because of the shortage or bitterness of the water, of God miraculously providing water, and etc....
It behooves all to take advantage of this heavenly blessing while we can. A time is coming when our water supply will be severely contaminated and eventually dried up. However it is during this time that God says to the righteous (right doers), "bread shall be given him; his waters [shall be] sure.[31] Notice that along with water, God also promised bread. This is significant! What is it about bread that God promises it in almost every case?

SOMETHING IN THE BREAD

Bread was associated with water as an article of food provided in dire times of necessity. What is it about bread that places it at a level with the most abundant nutrient known to man? This answer we will answer in several parts. First, bread is derived from grains, and grains were one of the subgroup foods given man at creation. Let us observe the chart. (See table 3)

Table 3		
The Original Diet		
Herb Bearing Seeds	Tree Yielding Fruit	Herb of Field
Grains	Fruit	Vegetables
Nuts		Legumes
Seeds		Tubers

Notice in the chart below that next to each subgroup is the most abundant nutrient in each group.

Subgroup Food	Major Macro Nutrient	Minor/Macro Nutrient	Minor/Macro Nutrient
Grains	Carbohydrates	Protein	Fat*
Nuts	Fat	Carbohydrates	Protein
Seeds	Fat	Carbohydrates	Protein
Fruits	Carbohydrates	Protein**	Fat**
Vegetables	Carbohydrates	Protein**	Fat**
Legumes	Carbohydrates	Protein	Fat**
Tubers (potatoes, and etc...)	Carbohydrates	Protein*	Fat**

* Low amount   **significantly low, and in most cases it is less than 1%

CARBOHYDRATES

Carbohydrates are unequivocally the most abundant solid nutrient in this chart. From a biblical and scientific perspective, any diet that belittles carbohydrates in general, and exalts proteins or fats in its place is not of God! Are we wiser than is our maker? Therefore, bread which is derived from grains is a part of the largest food group on most food pyramid, and is a staple article of food. Now there are different types of Carbohydrates.

Let us observe first, how carbohydrates are produced. "Carbohydrates are produced by green plants through a process known as photosynthesis. In the photosynthesis, a pigment called chlorophyll (pronounced KLOR-uh-fill) in the leaves of plants absorbs light energy from the Sun. Plants use this light energy to convert water and carbon dioxide from the environment into glucose and oxygen. Some glucose is used to form the more complex carbohydrate cellulose, the main structural component of plant cell walls. Some is used to provide immediate energy to plant cells. The rest is changed to a different chemical form, usually starch, and stored in seeds, roots, or fruits for later use.[32]

However, when we consider the biblical fact that states that the fruit, seeds, nuts, and etc. were actually created before the sun was created. This would indicate that carbohydrates such as fiber, sugar, and starches were at creation produced by God, and not the sun. God obviously created the sun to be a vehicle through which He would exercise His power as long as the earth should last. Even today God is exercising His power through the sun in producing carbohydrates. If God created carbohydrates, shall we not study His creative work!

Once again, the most abundant solid nutrient in the original diet is "carbohydrates". There are three types of carbohydrates. (See table 4)

Table 4		
Carbohydrates		
Single Sugars Also Called Monosaccarides	Bonded Single Sugars Also Called Disaccharides	Many/Complex Sugars Also Called Polysaccharides
Glucose	Glucose + Fructose = Sucrose	Glycogen
Fructose	Glucose + Galactose = Lactose	Fiber - Soluble - Insoluble
Galactose	Glucose + Glucose = Maltose	Starch
You will notice that "glucose" is the most abundant sugar in the diet.		

I will attempt to explain each briefly so that you can behold the intelligent design in carbohydrates, and its compatibility with the human machinery.

GLUCOSE is also called "blood sugar". The name "glucose" comes from the Greek word *glukus* meaning "sweet". The suffix "-ose" denotes a sugar. "Glucose, a monosaccharide (or simple sugar), is an important carbohydrate in biology. The living cell uses it as a source of energy and metabolic intermediate."[33] Among the various sugars, the body uses chiefly glucose directly as blood sugar to fuel the cells of the brain, nervous system, and tissues. It is absorbed rather rapidly into the blood stream. We will discuss later what controls the release of sugar in the blood stream.

"The brain and nervous system tissue use carbohydrates almost exclusively for energy"[34]
"Apparently as a result of the brain's very rapid metabolism, it is dependent on minute to minute supplies of this simple carbohydrate. This becomes easier to appreciate when you understand that the brain has a metabolic rate 7.5 times greater than the average body tissue."[35]

There are dogs that develop diabetes due to grain based diets. Dog's diet need to be protein and fat based. Humans conversely need a diet that is carbohydrate based. Humans have been created with higher powers of the mind (conscience, reason, choice, and etc...). The frequent use of these powers demands an abundant supply of carbohydrates in their diet to maintain proper brain and nervous system function. Of course, too much glucose is not good for the brain. It is with this delicate organ that God intends to lead us to salvation. When duty comes in contact with the mind, it lays burdens upon the conscience. God then says "Come now, and let us reason together... though your sins be as scarlet, they shall be as white as snow; though they be red like crimson, they shall be as wool."[36] After reasoning how sensible and loving the plan of salvation is, a voice comes home to the mind saying, "choose you this day whom ye will serve..."). Who will you choose? The choice is yours.

FRUCTOSE, also known as levulose, is a naturally occurring monosaccharide that can be found in fruits and honey. About twice as sweet as table sugar, and with a lower glycemic index... Fructose is atomically arranged different than glucose. This difference is what stimulates the taste buds on the tongue that produce the sweet sensation. Some diabetics use fructose in its free form because of its low glycemic index.* This however comes with its disadvantages. "Most of the carbohydrates we eat are made up of chains of glucose. When glucose enters the bloodstream, the body releases insulin to help regulate it. Fructose, on the other hand, is processed in the liver. *(It is processed the same way alcohol is processed. This can burden the liver.)* To greatly simplify the situation: When too much fructose enters the liver, the liver can't process it all fast enough for the body to use as sugar. Instead, it starts making fats from the fructose and sending them off into the bloodstream as triglycerides. A small amount of fructose, such as the amount found in most vegetables and fruits, is not a bad thing. In fact, there is evidence that a little bit may help your body process glucose properly."[37]

Fructose exists in foods as either a monosaccharide (free fructose) or as a disaccharide (sucrose). Free fructose does not undergo digestion; however when fructose is consumed in the form of sucrose, digestion occurs entirely in the upper small intestine. As sucrose comes into contact with the membrane of the small intestine, the enzyme sucrase catalyzes the cleavage of sucrose to yield one glucose and fructose unit. Fructose, passes through the small intestine, virtually unchanged, then enters the portal vein and is directed toward the liver.[38]

Some of the natural sources fructose are fruits, vegetables and honey. Fructose is often further concentrated from these sources. The highest dietary sources of fructose, besides pure crystalline fructose, are foods containing table sugar (sucrose), high-fructose corn syrup, agave nectar, honey, molasses, maple syrup, and fruit juices, as these have the highest percentages of fructose (including fructose in sucrose) per serving compared to other common foods and ingredients... In general, in foods that contain free fructose, the ratio of fructose to glucose is approximately 1:1; that is, foods with fructose usually contain about an equal amount of free glucose."[39] But, let it be remembered fructose is not blood sugar, and should not be consumed excessively, if at all in its free form. Excess fructose produces bloating and flatulence. If the glycogen stores are full, the body can store fructose as fat. We will discuss more about sugars later.

GALACTOSE is a monosaccharide. When united to glucose it forms lactose. Lactose is essentially milk sugar. Galactose is found in primarily in milk or milk products. This would include breast milk. Glucose can also be converted to galactose, which in turn enables the mammary glands to secrete lactose.

Galactose, like fructose, has the same chemical components as glucose but the atoms are arranged differently. The liver also converts galactose to glucose.[40] It has also been said that fructose and galactose were two of the best fermenting sugars in the absence of oxygen. Galactose comes from milk, and fructose is found either as a single sugar or as sucrose. The combination of these two sugars consumed in excessive amounts provides food for yeast. These yeasts consume these sugars, producing carbon dioxide and ethanol. This can lead beclouded mind. Anything that beclouds the mind makes it difficult to obey God.

SUCROSE is the combination of glucose and fructose joined together. It can be found in beet sugar, cane sugar, molasses, raw sugar, maple sugar, and white sugar. Sucrose needs to be digested before the body can utilize it. B-vitamins and calcium are needed to assist in digestion.

LACTOSE as mentioned before is a milk sugar. When God created mammals, He created them with mammary glands. Concerning humans, both men and women have mammary glands. They are formed during the embryonic stage. This is however the first phase of development. The second phase occurs during puberty in the female. Hormones initiate this development. Estrogen initiates further development whereas, in males this development is inhibited by testosterone. There is another development that occurs during pregnancy due to additional hormones called progesterone, prolactin, and other factors. This development stage prepares the female to be able to provide milk for a baby. After lactation, the breast pass trough what is called involution. Involution of an organ is the shrinking or return to a former size.

Humans are an exception in the natural world for consuming milk past infancy, despite the fact that many humans show some degree (some as little as 5%) of lactose intolerance, a characteristic that is more prevalent among individuals of African or Asian descent Asians and Africans represent at least 80% of the world's population. In America A quarter of the largest school districts.... offer rice or soy milk and almost 17% of all U.S. school districts offer lactose-free milk.[41]

After a child is weaned from milk, the body's lactose production decreases significantly. This continues as we age, especially after growing years. In reality lactose intolerance is a natural process. Further enzymes that break down protein decrease with age. This is especially the case with casein, which is a protein found abundantly in animal milk. "Human milk contains two types of proteins: whey and casein. Approximately 60% is whey, while 40% is casein. This balance of the proteins allows for quick and easy digestion. If artificial milk, also called formula, has a greater percentage of casein, it will be more difficult for the baby to digest. Approximately 60-80% of all protein in human milk is whey protein. These proteins have great infection-protection properties." This add is easier for the infant to digest.[42] In cow's milk approximately 82% of milk protein is casein, and the remaining 18% is serum or whey protein.[43]

MALTOSE is the combination of two glucose molecules. It is said to uncommon in nature but, can be formed by the break down of starch in the body. Barley is a known source of maltose after going through a process to produce "malt liquor".

GLYCOGEN is stored in the liver of living animals and living humans. It is essentially stored glucose. However, when an animal or human die, blood and oxygen supplies cease because the heart is no longer pumping blood to the tissues. "The decay of glucose in the absence of oxygen (anaerobic glucolysis) creates lactic acid."[44] Therefore, flesh foods are essentially wanting in the most abundant nutrient, "carbohydrates".

STARCHES are to plants, what glycogen is to the body, "stored energy". Starches are chains of glucose molecules joined together. When we consume the starches, they are broken down into glucose, and is either used immediately or stored in the liver or muscles. Excessive glucose will be stored as fat. Starches are mainly found in grains, tubers, legumes, and a few fruits such as bananas (contains 1-2% starch – but some is broken down as the banana ripens).

Grains are without rival, the most universal food used to satisfy energy and protein needs. So essential were grains in the Jewish economy that it was against the law to pledge a millstone. Said Moses, "No man shall take the nether or the upper millstone to pledge: for he taketh [a man's] life to pledge."[45] Millstones were used to grind grains as opposed to rolling grains, a technique used today. The rolling technique makes it easier to separate the endosperm from the bran, and the germ. These are then sold separately. Too much bran in this form is not the best. It contains a high amount of phytic acid, which can prevent the absorption of some minerals.

Grains have been shown to be a survival food. In the bible it was provided at different times in cases of famine, and it is also provided for the faithful followers of Christ at the end of this world. Amazing, God gives them a plant-based diet in the beginning of the world, and one at the end of the world. It is far inferior to that which was given at creation, but notice that grains and water are the only ones mentioned in the last diet. This is however, an "emergency diet", and is therefore temporary until after the translation of the saints. It is possible that the bread is cooked basing this on precedence. An angel baked grains for Elijah.[46] Below is a list of grains and their benefits. (See table 5)

LIST OF WHOLE GRAIN FOODS AND WHOLE GRAINS BENEFITS[47]

Table 5			
Whole Grain	Calories	Protein (g)	Carbs (g)
Amaranth	180	7	31
Barley Flakes	83	3	24
Barley, Hulled	176	5	39
Buckwheat	146	6	30
Couscous	180	7	31
Millet	150	3	24
Oats, Rolled	98	5	39
Oats, Steel Cut	170	6	30
Quinoa	120	7	31
Rice, Brown, Basmati	140	3	24
Rice, Brown, Long Grain	160	5	39
Rice, Brown, Medium Grain	160	6	30
Rice, Brown, Short Grain	180	7	31
Rice, Wild	160	3	24
Rye	160	5	39
Spelt	130	6	30
Wheat, Bulgur	150	7	31
Wheat, Durum	163	3	24
Wheat, Hard Red	160	5	39
Wheat, Soft Red	139	6	30
Wheat, Kernels	160	7	31
Whole Wheat Pasta (3/4 cup)	180	7	35

FIBER also called "roughage" is the indigestible portion of plant foods. Some animals possess microorganisms in the digestive tract that are able to break down the fiber. In the human body particularly the large intestines, bacteria are also able to break down the fiber (especially is the case with soluble fibers). The result is water, gas, and short chain fatty acids. This can be used as energy.

The foods that God gave man at creation contained fiber. In addition to the other benefits of the foods, fiber was essential to pushing out the byproducts of digestion. This would prevent straining, a habit so often practiced. This can result in painful hemorrhoids, or diverticulitis. More importantly, it would prevent foods from remaining in the colon to putrefy, become rancid, and or ferment. "When the bowels are not regularly pushing waste out, the entire digestive system can become backed up and unhealthy. Waste stays in our bodies longer, and becomes sticky and hardened along the intestinal wall, and, overtime, starts to fester and enlarge intestinal pores, letting toxins enter our blood stream."[48]

Constipation is considered to be the "mother of all diseases", because of the multiple affects that it can directly or indirectly have on the body "alone". Foods with no fiber, such as meat, should be avoided. Meat does not have any fiber. This would include all animal derivatives. Like humans, fiber passes through the gastrointestinal tract, and out of the body. In the stomach fibers have the ability to delay gastric emptying thus giving a feeling of fullness and satisfaction. The fibers also slow down the release of glucose into the bloodstream. Whole grains, and especially legumes and seeds, are excellent sources of fiber for diabetics. (See table 6)

Table 6			
Fibers: Their Characteristics, Food Sources, and Health Effects in the Body[49]			
Fiber Characteristics	**Major Food Sources**	**Actions in the Body**	**Health Benefits**
Viscous, soluble, more fermentable ▪ Gums and mucilages ▪ Pectins ▪ Psyllium ▪ Some hemicellulose	Whole-grain products (barley, oat bran, rye), fruits (apples, citrus), legumes, seeds and husks, vegetables; also extracted and used as food additives.	▪ Lower blood cholesterol by binding bile. ▪ slow glucose absorption ▪ slow transit of food through GI tract ▪ hold moisture in stools, softening them ▪ yield small fat molecules after fermentation that the colon can use for energy	▪ Lower risk of heart disease. ▪ Lower risk of diabetes.
Insoluble Fiber (not dissolvable) ▪ Cellulose ▪ Lignins ▪ Psyllium ▪ Resistant Starch ▪ Many hemicellulose	Brown rice, fruits, legumes, seeds, vegetables (cabbage, carrots, brussels sprouts), wheat bran, whole grains; also extracted and used as food additives	▪ Increase fecal weight and speed fecal passage through colon. ▪ Provide bulk and feelings of fullness	▪ Alleviate constipation. ▪ Lower risks of diverticulosis, hemorrhoids, and appendicitis. ▪ May help with weight management

GRAIN COOKING CHART[50]

1 cup Grain	Liquid	Cooking Method*	Cooking Time**	Yield (cups)
Amaranth	3	Simmer	15 min	2-2/3
Barley, grits	2/3	Cereal	3 min + 5 min standing time	2/3
Barley, hulled	4	Simmer	1 hour 45 min	2-1/2
Barley, pearl	3	Simmer	45-55 min	4
Barley, quick	2	Simmer	10-12 min	3
Buckwheat, groats, unroasted	2	Cereal	15 min	3-1/2
Buckwheat, groats, roasted'''	2	Cereal	15 min	3
Corn, meal	4	Cereal	10 min	3-1/2
Corn, hominy, dried	5	Simmer	5-6 hours	3
Millet	3	Simmer	25-30 min, 10 min standing time	5
Oats, quick	2	Cereal or steep	1 min + 3-5 min standing time	2
Oats, old-fashioned	2	Cereal	5 min	2
Oats, steel-cut	4	Cereal	20 min	2
Quinoa	2	Simmer	15 min	4
Rye, berries	3	Simmer	1 hour 55 min	3
Rye, flakes	3	Cereal	1 hour 5 min	2-1/2
Triticale, berries	3	Simmer	1 hour 45 min	2-1/2
Wheat, berries	3	Simmer	1 hour 10 min	2-1/2
Wheat, couscous	1-1/2	Steep	5-10 min	3
Wheat, cracked	2	Cereal	15 min	2
Wheat, flakes	4	Cereal	50-55 min	2
Wheat, bulgur	2	Steep	15 min	3

DEXTRINIZING

Dextrinizing is a process that involves toasting raw uncooked grains or flour in a skillet until slightly toasted. During this heating process starch molecules are broken down into smaller fragments called dextrin. The starch is essentially predigested making it easier to digest. The only disadvantage is that it does loose some of its nutrients due to the heat. Examples: lysine which is an amino acid, and vitamin B1.

FRUITS AND VEGETABLES

There should not be a great variety at any one meal, for this encourages overeating, and causes indigestion. It is not well to eat fruit and vegetables at the same meal. If the digestion is feeble, the use of both will often cause distress, and inability to put forth mental effort. It is better to have the fruit at one meal, and the vegetables at another. The meals should be varied. The same dishes, prepared in the same way, should not appear on the table meal after meal and day after day. The meals are eaten with greater relish, and the system is better nourished, when the food is varied.[51]

When students combine physical and mental taxation the objection to the third meal is to a great extent removed. Let the students have the third meal, prepared without vegetables, but with simple, wholesome food, such as fruit and bread.[52]

In the above counsel we find the reason why vegetables and fruit are best be eaten at separate meals. "If the digestion is feeble, the use of both will often cause distress, and inability to put forth mental effort."[53] The word "digestion" means the process by which food is broken down into absorbable units. Fruits as well as vegetables contain carbohydrates. One of the carbohydrates that are abundant in fruits and vegetables is fiber. Fiber is a complex carbohydrate that is indigestible by human enzymes. Some are broken down in the large intestines by the action of bacteria. As mentioned before there are two types of fibers: soluble & insoluble. The major sources of soluble fiber are fruits (apples, citrus), oats, barley, and legumes. If you stirred some soluble fiber into hot water, it would dissolve. In your stomach, the soluble fiber you've eaten dissolves in the water from your food and/or digestive juices and makes a viscous liquid or gel. When the fiber is dissolved it releases the sugars that are found in fruits. Since fruits are composed of essentially monosaccharides (single sugars) it is absorbed into the bloodstream in shorter period than most foods including vegetables. Bananas are an exception in that its carbohydrates are 1-2% starch. Vegetables conversely are considered to be a major source for insoluble fiber though vegetables can also contain some soluble fiber.

Fruits are considered to be the mature part of the plant. It contains little or no starch. This is due to the conversion of the starch into sugar during the maturation process. It needs no digestion since it is already in its simplest form, single sugar. However you do need to break down the fruit with your teeth, thus facilitating easier absorption. This is called mechanical digestion, and is accompanied by saliva that chemically digests starches and sugars. When fruit is eaten with vegetables, the vegetables can slow down the absorption of the sugars found in the fruits. These sugars do not need to stay long in the stomach. For good digestion they require only vitamins and enzymes and therefore spend a shorter time in the stomach. Therefore those whose digestion is feeble will act upon the vegetables much slower than normal resulting in fermentation, carbon dioxide and alcohol in the stomach. Carbon dioxide tends toward acidity in the stomach. Said one writer, "Fruit and vegetables taken at one meal produce acidity of the stomach; then impurity of the blood results, and the mind is not clear because the digestion is imperfect." You should understand that every organ of the body is to be treated with respect. In the matter of diet, you must reason from cause to effect."[54] For "perfect digestion" fruits and vegetables should be eaten at different meals. While some may have a better digestive system, the above counsel is the best way for all in assisting in "better digestion" and not "mediocre digestion".

Fruits are the mature part of the plant and have more sugar than vegetables. This is why diabetics can handle vegetables better than fruit. Fruits are broken down quicker and absorbed into the bloodstream.

VEGETABLES IN ITS VARIOUS FORMS ARE:

Leaves: lettuce, escarole, endive, etc
Fruit: tomatoes, cucumbers, peppers, avocado, etc*
Flowers: cauliflower, broccoli, artichoke

Stalks: asparagus, celery
Roots: carrots, red beets, etc
Bulbs: onions, garlic, fennel, etc.[55]

* Some fruit vegetables are considered by some to be fruits and others to be vegetables. But, these differences of opinions should not be made mountains. There is more to health reform, and a higher object than these minute differences. Let us do all that we can to answer the prayer of Christ found in John the 17th chapter.

Some vegetables are broken down much quicker than other vegetables. Vegetables in general contain more protein than fruit, and fruit generally contains less than 1 gram of protein. This would necessitate longer digestion.

VEGETABLES AND SWEET DESSERTS

Puddings, custards, sweet cake, and vegetables, all served at the same meal, will cause a disturbance in the stomach.[56]

OBSERVING REGULARITY

There has not been in this family the right management in regard to diet; there has been irregularity. There should have been a specified time for each meal, and the food should have been prepared in a simple form and free from grease; but pains should have been taken to have it nutritious, healthful, and inviting.[57] Well-ordered meals allow your digestive system to handle digestion more smoothly, with less time and more absorption of nutrients. A well ordered meal is one in which you introduce different foods systematically.
You should start by introducing the easiest or quickest to digest foods first and work your way up to the more complex. By doing this you keep foods that digest more easily flowing through your digestive system and prevent a "food traffic jam".[58]

The shape of the stomach allows food to be digested in the order that it comes into the stomach. Instead of a 100% vertical position in the stomach it has a slight slant so that food would go downward in an orderly fashion without breaking the ranks. It is slightly standing up and slightly sitting down. Taking this into consideration sitting, standing, and a light walking after eating are in harmony with the anatomy of the stomach. Sitting of course is acceptable, yet not the best initially, but perhaps after a brisk walk. However, sitting is far preferable to lying down.

Everyone has an internal clock and it is this internal clock that sets your body's rhythm. It is important that you set an eating schedule so that your body can maintain this rhythm. Your body becomes accustom to an eating schedule and starts producing digestive enzymes in preparation for food.

Your eating schedule should include both the times of day that you eat and the types of food groups that you eat (this includes fruits and vegetables). Eating odd foods or at odd times of day will disrupt your body's rhythm. When your rhythms are disrupted, your digestion is disrupted and the result is digestive discomfort.[59]

WHY EAT RAW FRUITS AND VEGETABLES FIRST?

- They provide digestive enzymes, and aid in the digestion of foods that have a higher content of major nutrients.
- It prevents inflammation in the intestines which occurs after beginning a meal with cooked food.
- Produce a greater feeling of satiety[60]

THE DANGERS OF IMPROPER EATING HABITS

I am astonished to learn that, after all the light that has been given in this place, many of you eat between meals! You should never let a morsel pass your lips between your regular meals. Eat what you ought, but eat it at one meal, and then wait until the next.

Many turn from light and knowledge, and sacrifice principle to taste. They eat when the system needs no food, and at irregular intervals, because they have no moral stamina to resist inclination. As the result, the abused stomach rebels, and suffering follows. Regularity in eating is very important for health of body and serenity of mind. Never should a morsel of food pass the lips between meals.[61]

When digestion in the stomach has been completed, the semi-liquid food is slowly released into the small intestines. For a time the stomach acts more like a storage for the semi-liquid food. Water can be taken at this time. However, food cannot. Food taken at this time will restart digestion all over again, and the food that should have been slowly released from the stomach remains until the food taken in between meals is digested. This can lead to fermentation foods.

EATING LATE BEFORE RETIRING

It is quite a common custom with people of the world to eat three times a day, beside eating at irregular intervals between meals; and the last meal is generally the most hearty, and is often taken just before retiring. This is reversing the "natural order"; a hearty meal should never be taken so late in the day. Should these persons change their practice, and eat but two meals a day, and nothing between meals, not even an apple, a nut, or any kind of fruit, the result would be seen in a good appetite and greatly improved health.[62]

Remember the anatomy of the stomach! During digestion sitting, standing, and light walking are in harmony with digestion. Lying down is not. Conversely when we are sleeping digestion should be complete. Lying down will then be in harmony with the stomach that is resting. In my estimation, 2-3 hours should follow a third meal. This is provided the third meal is in harmony with following paragraph.

Late eating of complex foods such as nuts, vegetables, beans, meat, cheese, causes the stomach that is ready to rest, to work over time with very little energy, and enzymes. Our bodies is said to produce 3 pints of enzymes per day. Approximately 1.5 is used during breakfast, and 1.5 during lunch. With this in mind the best food to eat would be foods containing their own enzymes, simple sugars & soluble fiber (fruits), and that are twice baked (breads, cereals). The starches in these foods are broken down to smaller fragments that are easier to digest. This would however, exclude bananas, coconuts, and dried fruits due to the higher content of sugar, fat, and or protein.

When students combine physical and mental taxation the objection to the third meal is to a great extent removed. Let the students have the third meal, prepared without vegetables, but with simple, wholesome food, such as fruit and bread.[63] You will notice that vegetables are not recommended for a third meal, but rather discarded.

Another pernicious habit is that of eating just before bedtime. The regular meals may have been taken; but because there is a sense of faintness, more food is taken. By indulgence this wrong practice becomes a habit and often so firmly fixed that it is thought impossible to sleep without food. As a result of eating late suppers, the digestive process is continued through the sleeping hours. But though the stomach works constantly, its work is not properly accomplished. The sleep is often disturbed with unpleasant dreams, and in the morning the person awakes unrefreshed and with little relish for breakfast. When we lie down to rest, the stomach should have its work all done, that it, as well as the other organs of the body, may enjoy rest. For persons of sedentary habits late suppers are particularly harmful. With them the disturbance created is often the beginning of disease that ends in death.[64]

TWO MEALS vs. THREE MEALS

Most people enjoy better health while eating two meals a day than three; others, under their existing circumstances, may require something to eat at supper-time; but this meal should be very light. Let no one think himself a criterion for all, — that every one must do exactly as he does.[65]

Three meals a day and nothing between meals--not even an apple--should be the utmost limit of indulgence. Those who go further violate nature's laws and will suffer the penalty.[66]

In many cases the faintness that leads to a desire for food is felt because the digestive organs have been too severely taxed during the day. After disposing of one meal, the digestive organs need rest. At least five or six hours should intervene between the meals, and most persons who give the plan a trial will find that two meals a day are better than three.[67]

The practice of eating but two meals a day is generally found a benefit to health; yet under some circumstances persons may require a third meal. This should, however, if taken at all, be very light, and of food most easily digested.[68]

LIQUIDS/SOLIDS/DIGESTION

Food should not be eaten very hot or very cold. If food is cold, the vital force of the stomach is drawn upon in order to warm it before digestion can take place. Cold drinks are injurious for the same reason; while the free use of hot drinks is debilitating. In fact, the more liquid there is taken with the meals, the more difficult it is for the food to digest; for the liquid must be absorbed before digestion can begin. Do not eat largely of salt, avoid the use of pickles and spiced foods, eat an abundance of fruit, and the irritation that calls for so much drink at mealtime will largely disappear. Food should be eaten slowly and should be thoroughly masticated. This is necessary in order that the saliva may be properly mixed with the food and the digestive fluids be called into action.[69]

"Many make a mistake in drinking cold water with their meals. Taken with meals, water diminishes the flow of the salivary glands; and the colder the water, the greater the injury to the stomach. Ice water or ice lemonade, drunk with meals, will arrest digestion until the system has imparted sufficient warmth to the stomach to enable it to take up its work again. Hot drinks are debilitating; and besides, those who indulge in their use become slaves to the habit. Food should not be washed down; no drink is needed with meals. Eat slowly, and allow the saliva to mingle with the food. The more liquid there is taken into the stomach with the meals, the more difficult it is for the food to digest; for the liquid must first be absorbed. Do not eat largely of salt; give up bottled pickles; keep fiery spiced food out of your stomach; eat fruit with your meals, and the irritation which calls for so much drink will cease to exist. But if anything is needed to quench thirst, pure water, drunk some little time before or after the meal, is all that nature requires. Never take tea, coffee, beer, wine, or any spirituous liquors. Water is the best liquid possible to cleanse the tissues."[70]

Ellen G. White does not specify how much time we should drink before or after a meal. But she gives us a principle. Today there are many schools of thought on this subject. A small number of authorities say that drinking water with your meal actually improves digestion. Some say that it is not healthy. There is no generic conclusion on this matter. However, I believe in the inspired writings, and all we need to do is to align it with the anatomy and physiology of the body. A study on digestion will bring some light. You can read this one for example on http://en.wikipedia.org/wiki/Digestion.

Proper digestion in the stomach needs activated enzymes. When masticated food enters the stomach, the stomach secretes proteases which are enzymes that digest proteins. Things that are needed for those enzymes to work properly are 1) hydrochloric acid, which has a pH 1-2, and 2) a certain temperature of the stomach.

The stomach also needs to churn and turn the food ingested to a more liquid state of what we call chyme. This process takes about 1-2 hours or 40 minutes to a few hours according to other authorities depending on the amount of food ingested. One thing that we need to keep in mind is that in gastric emptying, liquid form is emptied quicker than solid form. Liquids are normally emptied before solids.

When water is ingested too soon after a meal, the water will dilute the hydrochloric acid, which will impede enzyme action. And if the temperature of the water is cold, that will interfere as well. This water will be emptied first instead of the food, and thus delaying digestion. So we need to wait until the food in the stomach is in a more liquid form before we start drinking. At this point the digestive action of food in the stomach is turned off due to hormones, and the stomach becomes a little storage for the chyme until it is slowly & completely released into the small intestines. It is in the small intestines that 95% of absorption takes place.

BREAKFAST

APPLE OAT CRUMBLE

8 – 10 c. Granny Smith's apples or peaches
1 can apple juice concentrates
2 cans water
2 TBSP. vanilla flavor
1 tsp. cardamom
1 tsp. coriander
2 tsp. fresh lemon juice (omit when using Granny Smith's)

½ tsp. sea salt
1/3 c. honey (optional)
¼ c. cold water
¼ c. cornstarch
2 TBSP. non- hydrogenated butter
2x Oat Crumble recipe page 27

Combine all ingredients except for the last four ingredients. Bring to a boil, and then mix cornstarch and cold water together and pour it into the boiling water until it thickens. Add the butter and pour into a pan. Sprinkle over the top of the apples **the precooked Oat Crumble recipe 27**. Cook for 10 minutes at 350°.

ALMOND LEMON MILK

1 c. blanched almonds
4 c. water
2 TBSP. vanilla flavor
1-2 tsp. lemon rind

1 tsp. salt
1/3 c. maple syrup

In a small pot of boiling water, soak a cup of raw almonds for about 11-1/2 minutes. Afterwards, cool with cold water, and then take the skin off of the almonds. Blend all ingredients into 2 cups of water until smooth, and then add the remaining water. Use for cereals.

ALMOND SESAME SEED MILK

½ c. lightly roasted almonds
1 c. cashews
1 tsp. sea salt
¼ c. coconut milk

2 TBSP. lightly roasted sesame seeds
4 c. water
2 TBSP. vanilla flavor
½ -1 c. honey

Blend all ingredients thoroughly in 2 c. of the water. Next, add the rest of the water and blend for one minute.

BAKED OATS

3 c. boiling water
2 TBSP. shredded coconut, roasted
1 TBSP. vanilla flavor
½ tsp. coriander
¼ c. honey or more

2 c. oats
1 tsp. sea salt
¼ c. raisins
¼ tsp. cardamom
2 TBSP. soy powder

Mix all ingredients, except coconut, in a big bowl. Then pour into a pan, and cook at 350° for 1 hour. Sprinkle roasted coconut over, and serve with milk.

BLUEBERRY SAUCE 1

2 c. dates **or** 1 c. honey
5 c. frozen blueberries
6 TBSP. Arrowroot or cornstarch
2 TBSP. lemon juice

4 c. cold water
1 tsp. sea salt
2 TBSP. vanilla

Blend dates (if not using honey) with 2-3 of the cups of cold water in a blender thoroughly, and then add the extra cup of water and cornstarch. Mix the sweetener with all of the ingredients into a pot, and cook until thickened. Server over waffles, pancakes, etc.

BLUEBERRY SAUCE 2

10 c. frozen blueberries
2 cans of water (use the apple juice concentrate cans)
1 tsp. vanilla flavor

2 cans apple juice concentrate
Pinch of salt
½ c. Arrow root

Put all ingredients into a pot and mix together. Next, cook until thickened. Serve over waffles, French toast, or pancakes.

BLUEBERRY SAUCE 3

3 lbs. frozen blueberries
¼ c. Arrowroot

½ c. Xylitol
¼ c. cold water

Let the blueberries thaw out completely, and then put into a pot. Next, add water, and Arrowroot (thickener), and then cook until thickened. Do not over boil. If the blueberries are fully thawed out, omit the water, and then mix the Arrowroot with the blueberry juice before cooking. This is to as far as possible maintain the natural blueberry flavor.

BREAD PUDDING

2-½ -3 ½ c. of toasted bread (lightly buttered toasts)
1x Vanilla Pudding 2 page 81, or 1 pack Mori–Nu Vanilla Pudding® (from a health food store)
¼ tsp. of cardamom
1/3 c. raisins
¼ tsp. of coriander

Cut bread into 9 pieces, and layer in a pan. Mix raisins in with the bread. Mix spices with the pudding and pour over the bread. Make sure there is enough pudding to cover the entire dish. Let there be excess pudding in the bread pudding. Bake at 350° for 30 minutes.

BREAKFAST POTATOES

9 c. cubed potatoes (½ x ½ inches)
¼ c. yeast flakes
1 TBSP. garlic powder
1 tsp. sweetener
1 tsp. grounded dried red bell peppers or paprika

½ c. oil
2 TBSP. onion powder
2-3 tsp. sea salt
2 tsp. dried oregano leaves

Mix oil and potatoes together, and then add the rest of the ingredients. Bake in a covered casserole dish for 45 minutes–1 hour. Afterwards, remove covering, and let bake for 15 more minutes.

Tips: You may make your own paprika by dehydrating your own red peppers, and then ground in a blender to a powder.

BREAKFAST GRAVY

2 c. water
2 TBSP. flour (optional)
1 TBSP. onion powder
1 TBSP. yeast flakes

½ c. cashews
½ tsp. sea salt or to taste
½ tsp. Italian seasoning
Pinch of fennel seeds (optional)

Blend all ingredients thoroughly in a blender, except for Italian seasoning. Pour into a pot, and add Italian seasoning. Cook until thickened. Can be served over biscuits, rice, etc.

CALVIN'S CREPES

1 c. whole wheat flour
1 – 1½ c. water
¼ c. honey
½ tsp. sea salt

1 c. unbleached flour
½ c. oil
2 TBSP. vanilla flavor

In a bowl, mix all ingredients with the water. Add as much as needed until you have a pancake batter consistency. On a lightly greased skillet, pour ½ cup of batter, and cook until lightly brown on each side. Serve with fruit spread or syrup.

CALVIN'S GRANOLA

1 c. rolled oats
1 c. quick rolled oats
¼ c. sliced almonds
¼ tsp. salt
2 tsp. vanilla flavor
½ tsp. cardamom

1 tsp. almond flavor **or** 2 tsp. orange or lemon rind
¼ c. flour
½ c. evaporated cane sugar
1/3 – ½ c. oil
½ tsp. coriander
¼ tsp. Featherweight® Baking Powder

Mix all together and bake on a cookie sheet. Bake for 40 minutes to 1 hour at 350° stirring it every 5 minutes. DON'T LET OVERCOOK! It should have a slight golden, brown look. Let it sit until it becomes somewhat crunchy. For variation, mix ½ cup of healthy cornflakes and ½ cup of brown rice crispies.

CALVIN'S PANCAKES

1 ½ c. cold soy milk (add more if needed)
1/3 c. oil
1 ½ c. unbleached flour
3 tsp. Featherweight®

2 tsp. vanilla flavor
1 ½ t. salt
½ c. whole wheat flour
3 TBSP. honey or sweetener of choice

Sift salt and flour together. Mix oil and honey together, and then mix into flour. Mix Featherweight® in the mixture. Then, mix soymilk until pancake consistency. Pour and spread 1/3 cup of the batter onto sprayed pan, and cook both sides until lightly brown. For variation, add blueberries or pecans. This recipe can also be used as a waffle batter.

CASHEW MILK

1 c. cashews
1/3 c. honey
½ tsp. grated orange rind
½ -¾ tsp. salt

3 c. water
2 tsp. vanilla flavor
¼ tsp. coriander

Rinse the cashews. Blend all ingredients together thoroughly.

COCONUT OAT WAFFLES

3 c. oats
¼ c. coconut shredded
¼ c. flaxseeds
1 tsp. salt
4 TBSP. honey

3 c. water
¼ c. coconut oil
¼ c. walnuts
1 ½ TBSP. vanilla flavor
Small piece of orange peel

Blend all ingredients thoroughly. Pour 3/4-1 cup of the batter onto waffle iron, let cook for 6-10 minutes or until done. Put in the oven covered, so that it can remain hot and soft until ready to serve. You can also freeze them for later use.

CORNMEAL MUSH

1 c. cornmeal
3-4 c. cold water

¾ tsp. sea salt (minimal amount)

Mix cold water, salt, and cornmeal together in a pot. Turn the stove on high. Stir continually until the grits thicken. Once the grits are thickened, turn down to low and let cook until the grains are chewable. You may need to add more water. For variation, add coriander, cardamom, soy butter, sweetener, and coconut milk.

CORN OAT WAFFLES

2 c. oats
½ c. cornmeal
¼ c. almonds
1 ½ TBSP. vanilla flavor
¼ tsp. cardamom

3 c. water or more
¼ c. shredded coconut
½ tsp. sea salt
3 TBSP. honey
¼ tsp. coriander

Blend all ingredients thoroughly. Pour 3/4 cup of the batter onto waffle iron, let cook for 6-10 minutes or until done. Put in the oven covered, so that it can remain hot and soft until ready to serve. You can also freeze them for later use.

CREAM CHEESE SAUCE

2 c. oil
¾ c. sweetener
1-2 tsp. salt

1 ½ c. soy milk
1 tsp. vanilla flavor
2 of 8-oz. container of Tofutti® Cream Cheese

Blend in a blender. Next, put into a glass bowl and chill in the refrigerator.

OAT WAFFLES

2 ½ c. rolled oats
1 tsp. sea salt
3 TBSP. sweetener

¾ c. pecans
3 c. water
1 TBSP. vanilla flavor

Blend in a blender. Pour ¾ cup of the batter onto a round waffle iron, and cook until done.

FRENCH TOAST 1

1 c. soy milk or water
2-4 tsp. honey
1 tsp. flour
¼ tsp. coriander

¾ c. cashews
½ tsp. salt
2 tsp. vanilla flavor
¼ tsp. cardamom

Blend all ingredients and pour into a bowl. Dip some sliced bread into the batter wetting both sides. Bake at 350° on a sprayed sheet pan on each side until light brown. You can in a slightly greased pan, cook on the stove or cook on a waffle iron. Serve with fruit topping or maple syrup.

FRENCH TOAST 2

1 c. unbleached flour **or** whole wheat pastry flour
¼ c. oil (you can mix a little coconut oil into the oil mixture)
1 ¾ c. water
1 ½ TBSP. Featherweight®
¾ tsp. sea salt
1 tsp. vanilla flavor

3 TBSP. sweetener
1 TBSP. yeast flakes
½ tsp. liquid lecithin

Combine all ingredients together in a bowl. Dip a slice of bread into the batter. Put onto an oiled waffle iron, or lightly oiled skillet. Cook in the waffle iron for about 1-2 minutes. If cooking in a skillet, cook until golden brown on each side. This same batter can be used to make a waffle. Just pour ¾ -1 cup of batter onto the waffle iron. When using as a waffle batter, you may need to slightly decrease the water content.

HOMEMADE GOVERNMENT MARGARINE

¼ c. coconut milk
1 c. water
12 oz. silken tofu

½ c. soybean/safflower oil
½ c. lecithin granules
½ c. coconut oil (organic expeller cold press)

Blend all ingredients thoroughly. Pour into a mold dish that has been sprayed with oil spray. Let sit in refrigerated until firm.

LEMON MILK

1 x 1 inches lemon rind
1 c. cashews
2 TBSP. vanilla flavor
½ tsp. salt

4 c. water
½ c. soy powder
½ c. honey **or** a ½ c. dates
1/3 c. oil (optional)

Blend thoroughly one cup of cashews with 1 ½ cup water and lemon rind, then blend the rest of the ingredients thoroughly. Serve over cold or hot cereal.

LEMON MILLET PUDDING

4 c. cooked millet
2 TBSP. lecithin granules
½ tsp. cardamom
¼ c. coconut

2 ½ c. **Lemon Milk page 26** (more or less)
½ tsp. coriander
½ c. chopped walnuts
¼ c. honey (optional)

Blend half of the millet with some **Lemon Milk** and lecithin granules. In a big bowl, mix remaining ingredients together and bake in a baking dish in the oven at 350° for 30 minutes. You can sprinkle granola over the pudding.

HOMEMADE MAPLE SYRUP

2 c. water
1 TBSP. Arrowroot or cornstarch
1 ½ tsp. maple flavor

1 c. evaporated cane sugar
Pinch of salt

Cook on the stove until it thickens. You can also omit the maple flavoring and use as sweetener in cereals or drinks. This can help to cut down the amount calories per tablespoon of sweetener. You can add approximately ¼ cup of pure maple syrup.

MILLET PUDDING

2 c. cooked millet
2 bananas
½ tsp. salt
1 ½ TBSP. vanilla flavor

1 c. crushed pineapples
1 tsp. banana flavor (optional)
2 TBSP. honey
1x Oat Crumble recipe page 27

Mix together well and pour in a baking dish, next spread the precooked **Oat Crumble recipe** on top of the millet pudding. Bake for 10 minutes at 350°.

OAT CRUMBLE

2 c. rolled oats
½ c. flour
¼ - ½ c. evaporated cane sugar
½ tsp. sea salt
½ c. oil or non hydrogenated butter

¼ c. soy milk
2 tsp. vanilla flavor
1 tsp. coriander
1 TBSP. cardamom
¼ tsp. Featherweight®

Mix all together and bake on cookie sheet stirring periodically for 35 – 45 minutes at 350°.

OAT SAUSAGES 1

4 ½ c. boiling water
2 c. TVP (Texturized Vegetable Protein)
2 TBSP. garlic powder

3 ½ c. oats
¼ c. honey
3 TBSP. onion powder

½ c. yeast flakes   1½ TBSP. thyme
1 TBSP. sage   1 tsp. cumin
2 TBSP. oil   ½-¾ c. Braggs® **or** ¾ c. water+1¼ -1½ TBSP. of salt

Mix together and let sit for 20 minutes, then form into patties of your desired size. Bake on a sprayed pan for 40 minutes at 350°, turning over halfway. Note: TVP (Texturized Vegetable Protein) can be purchased at a health food store.

OAT SAUSAGES 2

½ c. sunflower seeds (grounded)	2 ¼ c. boiling water	1 - 2 tsp. salt
1 tsp. chicken style seasoning	¼ c. yeast flakes	2 ½ tsp. onion powder
1 TBSP. Bakon® Hickory Seasoning	1 tsp. basil	1 ½ tsp. sage
½ tsp. cumin	½ tsp. thyme	1 TBSP. dill seed
2 TBSP. olive oil or non-hydrogenated butter	2 ¼ c. oats	1 TBSP. maple syrup

Mix all ingredients together adding the boiling water last. Let it sit for 30 minutes in the refrigerator. Bake on a sprayed pan for 40 minutes (or less) turning over halfway.

RICE PUDDING

1½ c. cooked rice	2 tsp. vanilla flavor	1/8 tsp. cardamom
1/8 c. crushed pineapples	¼ c. honey	¼ tsp. coriander
2 TBSP. raisins	¼ tsp. salt	2 c. water
¼ c. chopped walnuts	½ c. cashews	

Mix first 4 ingredients in a bowl. Blend the rest of the ingredients thoroughly. Mix into rice and put in a small pan and bake at 350° for 30 minutes.

"ROMA" SOY MILK

4 c. water   1 TBSP. vanilla
1 c. soy supreme powder   ¾ tsp. salt
½ - 1 c. oil   2 TBSP. Roma® Coffee Substitute
¾ c. sweetener

Blend all ingredients together until smooth.

PINEAPPLE RICE

4 c. brown rice   ¼ tsp. coriander
8 c. water   ¼ tsp. cardamom
2 tsp. salt   2 TBSP. non hydrogenated butter
1 TBSP. vanilla flavor   2 – 4 TBSP. honey
½ tsp. turmeric   2 ½ c. pineapple chunks

Cook brown rice in 8 cups of water, salt, and turmeric. After cooked, add remaining ingredients. Serve with **Vanilla Pudding Recipe 2 on page 81** over the rice.

SCRAMBLED TOFU SPREAD

½ c. bread crumbs   ½ c. green olives chopped
½ c. **Real Mayo Salad Dressing page 39**   4 TBSP. honey

28

Mix all ingredients together and spread on toast with tomatoes, avocados, or your choice.

SCRAMBLED TOFU 1

1 lb. extra firm tofu, crumbled
1 TBSP. Chicken Style seasoning
1 TBSP. onion powder
4 TBSP. yeast flakes
1 tsp. garlic powder

1/8 tsp. turmeric
Pinch of cayenne pepper (optional)
½ tsp. salt or to taste
½ green bell pepper, diced
½ onion, diced
2 TBSP. soy butter

Sauté veggies, and then put the crumbled tofu and seasonings on top of the sautéed veggies. Cook in a sprayed or lightly greased pan until all flavors are blended and food is hot. Note that some extra firm tofu brands are not as firm as other brands.

SCRAMBLE TOFU 2

1 lb. tofu
2 tsp. garlic powder
2 tsp. onion powder
¼ c. yeast flakes
½ tsp. turmeric
2 tsp. Bakon® Hickory Seasoning

2 tsp. salt
Pinch of cayenne pepper (optional)
2 c. diced green peppers and onions
½ tsp. tarragon seasoning
2 TBSP. non-hydrogenated butter

Mash and crumble tofu. Combine all ingredients, and cook on the stove with a little water and olive oil. After it is cooked, add 2 teaspoon of non-hydrogenated butter. You also may add shredded vegan cheese.

SESAME SEED MILK

4 c. water
1 c. cashews
1/3 c. honey

1 tsp. salt
1 TBSP. vanilla flavor
1 TBSP. slightly roasted sesame seeds

Blend the cashews with 1 ½ cups of water first. After blending up thoroughly, add the rest of the ingredients and blend for 1 minute. You may need to blend longer depending on the type and strength of the blender.

SOY CREAM

2 c. water
1 c. soy supreme
1/3 c. honey
¼ tsp. salt

1 c. oil
½ tsp. almond flavor
1 ½ TBSP. vanilla flavor

Blend all ingredients thoroughly.

SOY BUTTER 1

½ - 1 c. Soy Supreme® powder

2 c. oil

½ c. water   2 tsp. -1 TBSP. salt
1 TBSP. liquid lecithin

Blend all ingredients thoroughly, and then spread on a toast, waffle, or your choosing.

SOY BUTTER 2

1 c. coconut butter   1 tsp. salt or to taste
½ c. soy milk   ½ c. lecithin granules **or** 1 TBSP. liquid lecithin
½ c. soybean oil
¼ c. Soy Supreme® powder

Blend all ingredients in a blender, except for the soy milk and soy flour. Make sure that the coconut oil is soft. Cook the soy flour and soymilk on the stove until thicken. Next, add to the blended mixture and blend again. After blending the mixture, pour it into a sprayed butter mold or mold of choice. Put into the freezer until firm. Afterwards, put into the refrigerator. Use for breads, pancakes, etc.

TOFU BUTTER

¼ c. coconut milk   1/2 c. lecithin granules
1 c. oil   12 oz. silken tofu
1 c. water   2 tsp. salt

Blend all ingredients thoroughly.

TOFU CREAM

2 c. water   2 of 12-oz. silken tofu
1 c. oil   2 TBSP. vanilla flavor
1 tsp. salt   ½ tsp. almond flavor
½ - ¾ c. honey
1 TBSP. lemon juice

Blend all ingredients thoroughly. Let chill in the refrigerator.

YELLOW GRITS

1 c. yellow grits
3-4 c. cold water (water amount depends on the coarseness of the grits and on your preferred consistency)
½ tsp. sea salt (minimal amount)

Mix cold water, salt and grits together in a pot. Turn the stove on high. Stir continually until the grits thicken. Once the grits are thick, turn down to low and let cook until the grains are chewable. You may need to add more water. You can add soy vegan cheese, chicken style flavor, soy butter, sweetener, or coconut milk.

THE ORIGINAL DIET - PLANT BASED

God gave our first parents the food He designed that the race should eat. It was contrary to His plan to have the life of any creature taken. There was to be no death in Eden. The fruit of the trees in the garden was the food man's wants required. God gave man no permission to eat animal food until after the flood. Everything had been destroyed upon which man could subsist, and therefore the Lord in their necessity gave Noah permission to eat of the clean animals which he had taken with him into the ark. But animal food was not the most healthful article of food for man.

In choosing man's food in Eden, the Lord showed what the best diet was; in the choice made for Israel He taught the same lesson. He brought the Israelites out of Egypt and undertook their training, that they might be a people for His own possession. Through them He desired to bless and teach the world. He provided them with the food best adapted for this purpose, not flesh, but manna, "the bread of heaven." It was only because of their discontent and their murmuring for the fleshpots of Egypt that animal food was granted them, and this only for a short time. Its use brought disease and death to thousands. Yet the restriction to a nonflesh diet was never heartily accepted. It continued to be the cause of discontent and murmuring, open or secret, and it was not made permanent.[1]

AUTHOR'S COMMENTS: The Bible does not specifically say that the people who populated the earth before the flood ate meat, but let us remember the words of Christ in Luke 17:26-29 "And as it was in the days of Noe, so shall it be also in the days of the Son of man. They did eat, they drank...until the day that Noe entered into the ark, and the flood came. Likewise also as it was in the days of Lot; they did eat, they drank... until God ...destroyed them all". We must make the application by observing the world today; there are similarities between our day and Noah's day.

After the flood the people ate largely of animal food. God saw that the ways of man were corrupt, and that he was disposed to exalt himself proudly against his Creator and to follow the inclinations of his own heart. And He permitted that long-lived race to eat animal food to shorten their sinful lives. Soon after the flood the race began to rapidly decrease in size, and in length of years. The diet appointed man in the beginning did not include animal food. Not till after the flood, when every green thing on the earth had been destroyed, did man receive permission to eat flesh.[2]

AUTHOR'S COMMENTS: It is important for the reader to understand that after the fall of man the only article of food that was introduce into mans diet was vegetables. As a result of the flood, this article of food was destroyed, and God said, "Every moving thing that liveth shall be meat for you; even as the green herb have I given you all things. But flesh with the life thereof, which is the blood thereof, shall ye not eat. And surely your blood of your lives will I require; at the hand of every beast will I require it, and at the hand of man; at the hand of every man's brother will I require the life of man." Genesis 9:3-5. Meat eating would not add to our lives, but take away from it. It was a substitute until the vegetables grew back. "Those who eat flesh are but eating grains and vegetables at second hand, for the animal receives from these things the nutrition that produces growth. The life that was in the grains and vegetables passes into the eater. We receive it by eating the flesh of the animal. How much better to get it direct, by eating the food that God provided for our use!"[3]

PLANT BASED FOODS SUPERIOR TO ANIMAL FOOD

	Plant Based	Animal Based
1	Vitamin & Minerals	Vitamins & Minerals (In smaller amounts w/ exception of liver)
2	Phytochemicals	No Phytochemicals
3	Fiber	No Fiber
4	Carbohydrates	No Carbohydrates
5	Digest well	Difficult for Digestion

There are other advantages, but I believe you get the picture. "Animal food was not the most healthful article of food for man."[4]

Upon their settlement in Canaan, the Israelites were permitted the use of animal food, but under careful restrictions, which tended to lessen the evil results. The use of swine's flesh was prohibited, as also of other animals and of birds and fish whose flesh was pronounced unclean. Of the meats permitted, the eating of the fat and the blood was strictly forbidden. Only such animals could be used for food as were in good condition. No creature that was torn, that had died of itself or from which the blood had not been carefully drained, could be used as food.

By departing from the plan divinely appointed for their diet, the Israelites suffered great loss. They desired a flesh diet, and they reaped its results. They did not reach God's ideal of character or fulfill His purpose. The Lord "gave them their request, but sent leanness into their soul." They valued the earthly above the spiritual, and the sacred preeminence which was His purpose for them they did not attain.[5]

AUTHOR'S COMMENTS: Have the thought ever come to your mind, Why did Israel complain to Moses about not having the foods that were eaten in Egypt after God had just destroyed some of the people because of their complaining? The Bible says, "And when the people complained, it displeased the LORD: and the LORD heard it; and his anger was kindled; and the fire of the LORD burnt among them, and consumed them that were in the uttermost parts of the camp. And the people cried unto Moses; and when Moses prayed unto the LORD, the fire was quenched. And he called the name of the place Taberah: because the fire of the LORD burnt among them. And the mixed multitude that was among them fell a lusting: and the children of Israel also wept again, and said, who shall give us flesh to eat? We remember the fish, which we did eat in Egypt freely; the cucumbers, and the melons, and the leeks, and the onions, and the garlic: But now our soul [is] dried away: there is nothing at all, beside this manna, before our eyes." Num.11:1-6. God continued to feed the Hebrew host with the bread rained from heaven; but they were not satisfied. Their depraved appetites craved meat, which God in His wisdom had withheld, in a great measure, from them. . . . Satan, the author of disease and misery, will approach God's people where he can have the greatest success. He has controlled the appetite in a great measure from the time of his successful experiment with Eve, in leading her to eat the forbidden fruit. He came with his temptations first to the mixed multitude, the believing Egyptians, and stirred them up to seditious murmurings.

They would not be content with the healthful food which God had provided for them. Their depraved appetites craved a greater variety, especially flesh meats. This murmuring soon infected nearly the whole body of the people. At first, God did not gratify their lustful appetites, but caused His judgments to come upon them, and consumed the most guilty by lightning from heaven. Yet this, instead of humbling them, only seemed to increase their murmurings."[6]

AUTHOR'S COMMENTS: Many do not understand the effect that meat has upon the nervous system. Studies have shown that the stimulating and satisfying effect that is often experienced after eating meat is not because of any properties of its protein, vitamins, or minerals, but because of a stimulant called HYPOXANTHINE.

"Hypoxanthine is found in the muscles of meat, and it increases in its concentration as it ages. Hypoxanthine, along with inosinic acid and guanylic acid have a chemical structure similar to that in caffeine in coffee, and theobromine in cocoa. These all are central nervous system stimulants that produce a sensation of vitality and energy which in many cases is simply a feeling. They are addictive, which may explain why Israel complained even after god bought judgments upon them."[7]

The lustful diet that is developed from meat eating, has the tendency to lead a person to rather continue partaking of flesh foods when they know that it has been linked to many conditions such as cancer, obesity, heart diseases, and even frontal lobe damage. Studies have shown that a chemical called arachidonic acid which is found in meats causes' frontal lobe damage over time. This is where man thinks, discern, decide, and where character is developed. In short, it is where we exercise the will, develop character, develop spiritually, and obey God. This is the only part of the body that needs both physical and spiritual food for thought. [8]

When the use of flesh food is discontinued, there is often a sense of weakness, a lack of vigor. Many urge this as evidence that flesh food is essential; but it is because foods of this class are stimulating, because they fever the blood and excite the nerves, that they are so missed. Some will find it as difficult to leave off flesh eating as it is for the drunkard to give up his dram; but they will be the better for the change. [9]

The Lord plainly told His people that every blessing would come to them if they would keep His commandments, and be a peculiar people. He warned them through Moses in the wilderness, specifying that health would be the reward of obedience. The state of the mind has largely to do with the health of the body, and especially with the health of the digestive organs. As a general thing, the Lord did not provide His people with flesh meat in the desert, because He knew that the use of this diet would create disease and insubordination. In order to modify the disposition, and bring the higher powers of the mind into active exercise, He removed from them the flesh of dead animals. He gave them angels' food, manna from heaven.[10]

AUTHOR'S COMMENTS: Unfortunately, many are suffering from cancer, because of a lack of knowledge, and will power. God said, "If thou wilt diligently hearken to the voice of the LORD thy God, and wilt do that which is right in his sight, and wilt give ear to his commandments, and keep all his statutes, I will put none of these diseases upon thee, which I have brought upon the Egyptians: for I [am] the LORD that healeth thee. Exodus 15:26 The Egyptians suffered from the same diseases that men suffer from today, only, new disease have developed since then (Also every sickness, and every plague, which is not written in the book of this law, them will the LORD bring upon thee, until thou be destroyed Deut 28:61). God said, "If we would do that which is right." Obviously, we are doing something wrong, but God can provide strength to resist the clamors of perverted appetite.

God gave His people permission to eat flesh after the flood, but he laid down some restrictions. Of the meats permitted, the eating of the fat and the blood was strictly forbidden along with other restrictions. God said, "The life of the flesh is in the blood" Leviticus 17:11 "Speak unto the children of Israel, saying, Ye shall eat no manner of fat, of ox, or of sheep, or of goat. "And the fat of the beast that dieth of itself, and the fat of that which is torn with beasts, may be used in any other use: but ye shall in no wise eat of it. For whosoever eateth the fat of the beast, of which men offer an offering made by fire unto the LORD, even the soul that eateth it shall be cut off from his people. Moreover ye shall eat no manner of blood, whether it be of fowl or of beast, in any of your dwellings." Leviticus 7:23-26 "And ye shall be holy men unto me: neither shall ye eat any flesh that is torn of beasts in the field; ye shall cast it to the dogs." Exodus 22:31 That which dieth of itself, or is torn with beasts, he shall not eat to defile himself therewith: I [am] the LORD." Leviticus 22:8 "And if ye offer a sacrifice of peace offerings unto the LORD, ye shall offer it at your own will. It shall be eaten the same day ye offer it, and on the morrow: and if ought remain until the third day, it shall be burnt in the fire. And if it be eaten at all on the third day, it is abominable; it shall not be accepted. Leviticus 17:11, 7:23-26; Exodus 22:31; Leviticus 22:8, 19:5-7

Let us explore the reason why God laid down these restrictions. God did not flip a coin to distinguish whether or not something was clean or not clean.

GOD'S REASON FOR RESTRICTING THE USES OF:

BLOOD – The bible says that the life of the flesh is in the blood. "Often animals are taken to market and sold for food, when they are so diseased that their owners fear to keep them longer. And some of the processes of fattening them for market produce disease. (Many HORMONES and DRUGS are used to fatten cattle for the market by putting them in their feed, and the people who eat the meat get them in their system. People who have ingested a lot of hormones from meat eating often have a puffy appearance. One of those drugs used for fattening cattle and chickens today is diethyl stilbestrol, which has been shown to be carcinogen. It has produced cancer in humans who ate such meat. Divine Prescription Gunther B. Paulien, Ph.D p. 219) Shut away from the light and pure air, breathing the atmosphere of filthy stables, perhaps fattening on decaying food, the entire body soon becomes contaminated with foul matter. Animals are often transported long distances and subjected to great suffering in reaching a market. Taken from the green pastures and traveling for weary miles over the hot, dusty roads, or crowded into filthy cars, feverish and exhausted, often for many hours deprived of food and water, the poor creatures are driven to their death, that human beings may feast on the carcasses. Many do not know that it is the uric acid in the meat that gives it its taste. Uric acid is the by-product of protein metabolism. It is the kidneys job to remove this uric acid, but when the kidneys fail to perform its task, the uric acid is stored in the kidneys causing kidney disease, or bladder stones...The kidneys of a dog which we can classify as meat eater, has 10 times the capacity to eliminate uric acid than man.[11]

The Bible says, "And ye shall be holy men unto me: neither shall ye eat any flesh that is torn of beasts in the field; ye shall cast it to the dogs." Deut 22:31. Ammonia is another by-product of protein that breaks down the pancreas and lowers our resistance to cancer and prepare the way for diabetes.[12]

Many die of disease caused wholly by meat eating; yet the world does not seem to be the wiser. Animals are frequently killed that have been driven quite a distance for the slaughter. Their blood has become heated. They are full of flesh, and have been deprived of healthy exercise, and when they have to travel far, they become surfeited and exhausted, and in that condition are killed for market. Their blood is highly inflamed, and those who eat of their meat, eat poison. Some are not immediately affected, while others are attacked with severe pain, and die from fever, cholera, or some unknown disease. Very many animals are sold for the city market known to be diseased by those who have sold them, and those who buy them are not always ignorant of the matter. Especially in larger cities this is practiced to a great extent, and meat eaters know not that they are eating diseased animals.

Some animals that are brought to the slaughter seem to realize by instinct what is to take place, and they become furious, and literally mad. They are killed while in that state, and their flesh is prepared for market. Their meat is poison, and has produced, in those who have eaten it, cramps, convulsions, apoplexy, and sudden death. Yet the cause of all this suffering is not attributed to the meat. Some animals are inhumanly treated while being brought to the slaughter. They are literally tortured, and after they have endured many hours of extreme suffering, are butchered. Swine have been prepared for market even while the plague was upon them, and their poisonous flesh has spread contagious diseases, and great mortality has followed.[13]

FAT - Studies have shown that cholesterol is found only in animal foods. Most Americans get their cholesterol from meats 35%, eggs 35%, and dairy products 16%, cooking oils 6% (mainly from animals in origin such as, butter, lard, and other fats), and pastries.

It is important to recognize that the liver manufactures enough cholesterol for the whole body; this would make cholesterol in the diet unnecessary. The diet that God gave to Adam and Eve did not contain any cholesterol whatsoever.

The fats in meats are mainly saturated. Fish on the other hand is has been known to have a good source of polyunsaturated fats. However, there are some disadvantages. (Author's Comments: Remember that everything that has a liver has cholesterol) Fish can be beneficial to the health when it replaces the meat and not an addition to meat. "This would defeat the purpose because of the high amount of saturated fat or hydrogenated fats which add hydrogen atoms to the unsaturated fat making it more saturated. This is also the case with heated unsaturated fats such as in frying. The beneficial effects of fish are inferior to the foods that God has provided for mankind such as walnuts, soy products, and especially flax seeds.[14] Fish is contaminated with mercury, bacteria, and high in salt when used as a preservative.[15]

Our body does need fat. It is the type of fat that consumed that makes the difference. "Fats are important for are health. They help the balance the body's chemistry and provide padding as protection for vital organs.

34

They also provide a source of energy for body processes, and they help with the transportation of and absorption of fat soluble vitamins A, D, E, and K. They are also a source of the vital nutrients known as essential fatty acids. Some fats the body can synthesize, but the ones that can not be synthesized by the body have to be obtained through the diet, these are essential fatty acids. These fatty acids help with lowering triglycerides levels, remove plaque from the walls of the arteries, lowering blood pressure, etcetera.[16]

All vegetable oils are mainly unsaturated fats (Poly & Mono – Unsaturated Fats) with exception of coconut & palm oil. The fats in animals are mainly saturated.[17]

It is this type of fat that raises the cholesterol levels (LDL- Low Density Lipo-proteins), while unsaturated fats lower LDL levels by in HDL levels (High Density Lipo-protein). Excess fat is stored in the liver, in arteries, around the heart, and in tissues.[18]

Processed foods such as fish, meats, and etcetera may contain sodium without the chloride which lessens the salt taste. They normally are high in sodium and low, if any, in potassium which both are needed to balance the amount of sodium and potassium in the cell.

"There are other foods that contain harmful cholesterol by-products, which are harmful to our bodies. Cholesterol exposed to the atmosphere for a period of time tends to bind with oxygen in the air, producing what is called "oxidized cholesterol". Some of the chemicals called "oxidation products," were so toxic that they destroyed cells that line the arteries in less than 24 hours. Furthermore it took only a small amount of these toxic chemicals to cause irreversible damage. Studies have shown that when rabbits were given non-oxidized cholesterol in their diets for 45 days, their blood cholesterol levels stayed normal. When they were given the same amount of oxidized cholesterol their blood cholesterol levels were the same. However, they sustained significant damage to their blood vessels. Research on humans also supports the fact that oxidized cholesterol in the diet can increase your risk of heart disease even if your blood cholesterol levels stay normal. Atherosclerosis often begins early in life. Why? Well, research has shown that a baby that gets their milk from the mother's breast does get cholesterol, but not oxidized cholesterol. Cow's milk based formulas have oxidized cholesterol because they have been processes in the presence of air. Foods that have the combination of sugar, milk, eggs, and saturated oils are harmful. Also, other sources of the most harmful cholesterol are, pancake mixes, custard mixes (eggs is the chief ingredient), lard, and parmesan cheese."[19]

"Studies have shown two hard-boiled eggs increased HDL cholesterol levels by 10%, and rendered only a slight increase in total cholesterol by 4%. (Of course, this would be different if they were fried.) This and other discoveries confirm that the moderate use of eggs does not increase blood cholesterol levels. However, it does promote Arteriosclerosis to a great degree. It is initiated by the oxidation of LDL cholesterol the substance that transports cholesterol. Studies have shown that two eggs a day for three weeks increases oxidation of plasma lipoproteins by 42%. Eggs are responsible for 67% of all food – related poisonings. Foods such as mayonnaise is made with a raw egg and is a excellent medium for the development of microorganisms. Bacteria can still penetrate the eggs through its pores, especially if it is cracked. The longer an egg is stored the greater the possibility that bacteria have developed in its interior."[20]

SAUCES

ALMOND FRENCH DRESSING

¾ c. blanched almonds
1/3 c. lemon juice
¼ c. honey
1 c. lightly steamed carrots
2 slices of beets (from the can)

2 TBSP. onion powder
½ tsp. garlic powder
1 tsp. salt
¾ c. water

Bring almonds to a boil in a pot of water and boil for 1 minute. Next, strain the water and cool off with cold water and strip off the skin. Lastly, blend with all the ingredients in a blender thoroughly.

BAR B QUE SAUCE 1

29-oz. can tomato sauce
1 ½ TBSP. onion powder
1 ½ tsp. garlic powder
½ tsp. basil
½ tsp. salt
¾ c. Grandma's molasses (1/3 c. if using Blackstrap molasses)

1 TBSP. Braggs® Liquid Aminos
4 TBSP. lemon juice or more
2/3 c. honey
2 TBSP. non-hydrogenated butter
3 TBSP. Bakon® Hickory Seasoning

Place all ingredients into a pot and simmer.

BAR B QUE SAUCE 2

2 c. water
2 c. tomato sauce
¾ c. sweetener
½ c. oil
¼ c. Braggs® Liquid Aminos (more if desired)
¼ c. Arrowroot + ¼ c. water
¼ c. lemon juice

2 TBSP. Blackstrap molasses
1 tsp. basil
1 tsp. Roma® Coffee Substitute
½ tsp. sea salt
1 TBSP. onion powder
1 TBSP. garlic powder

Combine all ingredients into a pot, except for the oil. Allow to simmer for at least 30 minutes. Afterwards, add oil and cook for 5 minutes.

CASHEW MAYO DRESSING

12 oz. silken tofu
½ c. cashews
2 TBSP. onion powder
2 c. soy milk

2 tsp. sea salt
1 TBSP. honey

Blend all ingredients thoroughly.

CALVIN'S RANCH DRESSING

1 ¼ - 1 ½ c. water
1 ½ c. oil
¾ c. cashews
1 TBSP. sea salt

1 TBSP. onion powder
1 tsp. garlic powder
3 TBSP. evaporated cane juice
½ c. fresh lemon juice

Blend all ingredients thoroughly, except for the oil and lemon juice. Once it is well blended, pour the oil into the blender slowly while blending. Lastly, pour the lemon juice into the blender slowly while blending.

COUNTRY GRAVY

4 c. water
1 c. cashews
¼ c. Braggs® Liquid Aminos
1 tsp. sea salt (or to taste)
¼ c. flour
1 bay leaf

1 tsp. sage
2 TBSP. garlic powder
2 TBSP. onion powder
2 c. diced onions

Blend all ingredients except for onions in a blender with 2 cups of water. Once blended, pour into a pot with the rest of the water and onions.

ELIZABETH'S ITALIAN DRESSING

1 c. lemon juice
1 ½ c. olive oil
½ c. yeast flakes
1 ½ TBSP. onion powder
1 TBSP. Chicken Style Seasoning

1 TBSP. sea salt
1 tsp. garlic powder
4 TBSP. honey or to taste
2 tsp. Italian seasoning

Blend thoroughly for about 2 minutes, and then serve with salad.

FRENCH DRESSING 1

1 c. oil
1 ½ tsp. onion powder
1/3 c. lemon juice
1 ½ tsp. sea salt
1 TBSP. paprika

½ tsp. garlic powder
½ c. honey (or desire)
¾ c. tomato sauce
¼ fresh red bell pepper
1 ½ tsp. Bakon® Hickory Seasoning

Blend all ingredients thoroughly.

FRENCH DRESSING 2

1 c. cashews or sunflower seeds
1 of 15-oz. can tomato sauce
1/2-2/3 c. lemon juice
1 fresh onion
1 tsp. garlic powder

2 TBSP. onion powder
1 ½ TBSP. paprika
1 ½ tsp. sea salt
1 ½ c. water
1/3 c. honey

Blend all ingredients thoroughly.

GARLIC BREAD SAUCE

2 c. olive oil
¼ c. garlic powder
2 tsp. sea salt
¼ c. yeast flakes

1 TBSP. basil
1 TBSP. liquid lecithin
1 t. butter flavor (optional)

Blend all ingredients in a blender until it slightly creams up. Spread onto a slice of toasted bread and serve with spaghetti or dish of your choice. You may have to stir it before spreading onto bread.

ITALIAN DRESSING

1 ¼ c. lemon juice
¼ c. pineapple juice
1 c. olive oil
½ c. yeast flakes
3 tsp. Italian seasonings

½ tsp. garlic powder
1 TBSP. onion powder
2 TBSP. Chicken Style Seasoning
1 TBSP. honey
1 ½-2 ½ tsp. sea salt

Blend all ingredients together until creamy.

MAYO DRESSING 1

1/2 c. cashews
1 c. soy milk or water
6 oz. silken tofu (firm)
1/4 c. fresh lemon juice

1 1/4 tsp. sea salt or to taste
1 1/2 tsp. garlic powder
1 TBSP. onion powder

Blend everything together except lemon juice. Once blended thoroughly, add lemon juice. For ranch dressing, add 2 Tablespoon of honey and 1 Tablespoon of basil.

MAYO DRESSING 2

2 c. soy milk
1 c. oil
1 TBSP. sea salt
3 TBSP. sweetener

1 TBSP. onion powder
3 fresh garlic cloves
Pinch of caraway seeds

Blend all ingredients except for the water. Slowly add the soy milk till the desired consistency is reached.

PIZZA SAUCE

1 of 6-oz. can of tomato paste
1 tsp. Italian seasoning
2 TBSP. onion powder

2 TBSP. olive oil
1 tsp. sea salt
½ c. water

Mix together in bowl. Spread as much as needed over a pizza dough.

PIZZA TOPPING

¼ c. walnuts
½ tsp. sea salt
1 tsp. Italian seasoning

1 TBSP. yeast flakes
1 TBSP. garlic powder

Ground in a small processor. Sprinkle over some vegan cheese (Daiya® vegan cheese).

RANCH DRESSING

1/2 c. cashews or sunflower seeds
1 c. water
12 oz. silken tofu (firm)
1/3 c. lemon juice
1 1/4 tsp. sea salt
1 1/2 tsp. garlic powder

1 1/2 TBSP. onion powder
1 TBSP. honey
1 1/2 tsp. basil
1 1/2 tsp. oregano
1/4 c. olive oil {optional}

Blend all ingredients thoroughly.

REAL SALAD DRESSING

1 ½ c. soy milk (cold)
1 c. oil (more if needed)
1 TBSP. onion powder
1 TBSP. garlic powder
1/8 tsp. celery seed

2 tsp. salt
¼ c. lemon juice
¼ c. honey
2 – 4 TBSP. lecithin granules (optional)

Pour all ingredients into a blender. While these ingredients are blending, pour the soy milk into the blender slowly until thick. Use for macaroni salad, burgers, salads, etc. For ranch dressing, add 1-2 teaspoon of Italian seasoning.

SALAD DRESSING

½ lb. tofu
1/3 c. cashews
1 ½ tsp. sea salt
1 t. lecithin granules
¼ c. oil

¼ c. lemon juice
¼ c. honey
¼ c. water
2 tsp. garlic powder

Blend thoroughly until very smooth.

SOY MAYO

2 ½ c. water
½ -1 c. Soy Supreme® powder
½ c. sunflower seeds
¼ c. fresh lemon juice
1 ½ tsp. sea salt

2 TBSP. onion powder
1 TBSP. garlic powder
1/8 tsp. celery seed
2 TBSP. honey (more if desired)
2 TBSP. olive oil (optional)

Blend all ingredients thoroughly.

SOUR CREAM DRESSING

2 ½ c. water
¾ -1 c. sunflower seeds
½ c. lemon juice
½ c. olive oil
1 tsp. sea salt

3 TBSP. onion powder
2 TBSP. garlic powder
1 tsp. honey
1/8 tsp. celery seed

Blend all ingredients thoroughly.

SPAGHETTI SAUCE

4 of 8-oz. cans tomato sauce
1 of 6-oz. can tomato paste
1 TBSP. lemon juice
½ c. pineapple juice
1 green pepper
2 large onions
2 cloves garlic

1 tsp. sea salt
1 TBSP. Beef Style Seasoning (optional)
1 tsp. oregano
1 tsp. basil
¼ c. honey
1 TBSP. molasses

Sauté all veggies. Pour tomato sauce and paste, seasonings, sweeteners, and lemon juice into pot, and add the sautéed veggies. Bring to a boil and then simmer for 45 mnutes.

SUNFLOWER SEED DRESSING 1

2 ½ c. water
1 c. sunflower seeds
1/3 c. lemon juice
½ c. oil

1 TBSP. sea salt
3 TBSP. onion powder
2 TBSP. garlic powder
1/8 tsp. celery seed

Blend all ingredients thoroughly, and serve over salad.

SUNFLOWER SEED MAYONNAISE 2

2 c. oil
2 c. water
1 c. raw sunflower seeds
½ c. lemon juice

3 TBSP. sweetener
2 tsp. sea salt
1 TBSP. garlic powder

Blend thoroughly until smooth.

SUNNY SAUCE

1 c. cashews or sunflower seeds
2 of 15-oz cans tomato sauce
¼ c. lemon juice

2 ¼ tsp. sea salt
1 ½ tsp. onion powder
1 TBSP. yeast flakes

Blend thoroughly.

SWEET AND SOUR SAUCE 1

½ c. fructose or honey
2 TBSP. Blackstrap molasses
½ c. lemon juice
1 ½ tsp. garlic powder

1 ½ c. pineapple juice or orange juice
1 jar apricot, peach, or orange Polaners® jelly (optional)

1 TBSP. onion powder
3 TBSP. cornstarch
¼ - ½ c. Braggs® or salt to taste
1/8 tsp. celery seed (optional)

Blend the cornstarch with pineapple juice. Pour into a pot and add the rest of the ingredients, except for the Braggs. Heat until thickened. Let cool down, and then add Braggs.

SWEET AND SOUR SAUCE 2

3c. sugar
1 ½ -2 c. Braggs®
1 of 16-oz. can tomato sauce
1 c. lemon juice or orange Juice
½ c. yeast flakes
½ c. Arrowroot or cornstarch

½ c. water (optional if you mix starch into the mixture before cooking)
½ c. oil
¼ c. toasted sesame seeds **or**
      1 TBSP. sesame seed oil
2 TBSP. onion powder

Mix all together in a pot, except for oil, and then cook until thickened. If using Arrowroot, do not over boil it. Once it is thickened, turn off the stove. Next, add oil, and then pour over sliced firm water packed or vacuumed packed tofu. This recipe is good for about 8 lbs. of tofu. You do not have to use it all at one time.

TOFU MAYO

12 oz. firm silken tofu
1 TBSP. garlic powder
1 TBSP. onion powder
2-3 tsp. sea salt

¼ c. lemon juice
1 ¼ c. water
1/8 tsp. celery seed

Blend all ingredients thoroughly.

TOFU RANCH

1 ½ c. oil
1 ½ c. soy milk
12 oz. silken tofu
1/3 – ½ c. lemon juice
½ c. honey

1 TBSP. sea salt or to taste
2 TBSP. garlic powder
1 TBSP. Italian seasoning
½ tsp. Bakon® Hickory Seasoning

Pour all the ingredients into a blender, except for the silken tofu, and the pour milk into the blender slowly while it is blending. Next, put the silken tofu into the blender.

TOMATO HAWAIIAN SWEET & SOUR SAUCE

1 c. water
½ c. pineapple juice
½ c. lemon juice

¼ - ½ c. Braggs®
½ c. Grandma's molasses
1/8 c. tomato paste

½ c. pimentos
1 TBSP. onion powder
1 ½ TBSP. garlic powder
1/16-1/8 tsp. celery seed (optional)

3 TBSP. cornstarch
2 TBSP. yeast flakes
½ TBSP. Bakon® Hickory Seasoning
4 T. 1 jar of peach or orange Polaners® jelly

Whip all ingredients in a pot, except for Braggs. Cook until thick and pour over plain rice or rice mixed with soy curls or tofu. Soy curls can be purchased at some of your health food stores. You can also simmer the sauce with soy curls or tofu for about 25 minutes. After it is finished cooking, add the Braggs, then serve over rice or pasta.

TOMATO JUICE FRENCH DRESSING

4 c. tomato juice
½ - ¾ c. cashews
2 TBSP. paprika
3 TBSP. onion powder
1 ½ TBSP. garlic powder

1/3 – ½ c. fresh squeezed lemon juice
1 TBSP. sea salt
½ - ¾ c. honey
¼ c. olive oil (optional)

Blend all ingredients together thoroughly.

POPCORN SEASONING

¾ c. yeast flakes
1 ½ TBSP. onion powder
1 ½ TBSP. garlic powder
1-1 ¼ tsp. sea salt
1 tsp. basil

1 tsp. Paprika (fresh dehydrated, grounded red bell peppers)
1-2 tsp. lecithin granules
1 tsp. Chicken Style Seasoning
½-1 tsp. evaporated cane juice

Blend all ingredients into powder. Spray a little olive oil on your popcorn, and then sprinkle popcorn seasoning.

SPAGHETTI TOMATO SAUCE

9 of 15- oz. cans tomato sauce
2 TBSP. Italian seasoning
1 of 6-oz. can tomato paste
2 TBSP. lemon juice
2 green pepper diced
2 large onions diced
¼ c. onion powder
¼ c. garlic powder

2 tsp. sea salt
¼ c. Beef Style Seasoning
1 tsp. oregano
½ tsp. rosemary
1 ¼ c. honey
1 TBSP. Blackstrap molasses
1 ¼ olive oil

Sauté all veggies. Pour tomato sauce and paste, seasonings, sweeteners, and lemon juice into pot and add the sautéed veggies. Bring to a boil, and then simmer for 1 hours.

Our Creator created man from the dust of the ground. This dust is composed of elements that make up the human body. One of these elements is "nitrogen". Nitrogen is one of the distinctive atoms that separate protein from carbohydrates and fats.

* PROTEIN: CARBON, HYDROGEN, OXYGEN, NITROGEN, AND SOMETIMES SULFUR
* CARBOHYDRATES: CARBON, HYDROGEN, AND OXYGEN
* FAT: CARBON, HYDROGEN, AND OXYGEN

These nitrogen atoms give the name amino (nitrogen containing) to the amino acids-the links in the chains of proteins.[1] There are approximately 20 amino acids some of which is considered to be essential or non-essential. Essential amino acids are those that need to be obtained from the diet, and the non-essential amino acids are those that can be synthesized by the body.

Every cell and tissue in the body contains protein. It is in the muscles, bones, hair, nails and skin, accounting for 20 percent of total body weight. In addition, different proteins work as enzymes, hormones, neurotransmitters, antibodies and specialized proteins such as hemoglobin and others, constantly repairing body tissues to keep it healthy.[2]

We obtain protein from foods. Proteins, like carbohydrates, and fats are synthesized in plants. "Bacteria of the genus Rhizobium develop in their (legumes) roots. These have the capability to convert atmospheric nitrogen, an inert gas, into nitrogenous compounds such as ammonia and nitrates. The plant absorbs these compounds, which are then used to synthesize proteins"[3] However, in the cultivation of other plant based foods, nitrogenous substances are normally added to the soil a couple of weeks after planting. At any rate, the roots absorb the nitrogen to form proteins.

If we go back to creation we find on record these words, "And out of the ground made the LORD God to grow every tree that is pleasant to the sight, and good for food; the tree of life also in the midst of the garden, and the tree of knowledge of good and evil."[4] God's creative power is revealed in causing the vegetation to grow. "And Jesus bids us "consider the lilies how they grow."[5] The plants and flowers grow not by their own care or anxiety or effort, but by receiving that which God has furnished to minister to their life... The plant... grows by receiving from its surroundings that which ministers to its life --air, sunshine, and food (elements).6 supplied word "It is not because of inherent power that year by year the earth produces her bounties and continues her motion around the sun... It is through His power that vegetation flourishes, that the leaves appear and the flowers bloom. He "maketh grass to grow upon the mountains" (Psalm 147:8), and by Him the valleys are made fruitful. "All the beasts of the forest . . . seek their meat from God," and every living creature, from the smallest insect up to man, is daily dependent upon His providential care. In the beautiful words of the psalmist, "These wait all upon Thee. . . . That Thou givest them they gather: Thou openest Thine hand, they are filled with good." Psalm 104:20, 21, 27, 28. His word controls the elements; He covers the heavens with clouds and prepares rain for the earth. "He giveth snow like wool: He scattereth the hoarfrost like ashes." Psalm 147:16. "When He uttereth His voice, there is a multitude of waters in the heavens, and He causeth the vapors to ascend from the ends of the earth; He maketh lightnings with rain, and bringeth forth the wind out of His treasuries." Jeremiah 10:13. GOD IS THE FOUNDATION OF EVERYTHING![7]

With this weight of strong evidence, it is clear; proteins and all other nutrients are the handiwork of God, a revelation of His power! God at creation created the vegetation for all His creatures. Man and beast received their protein from plant based foods. After sin, some animals became carnivorous creatures eating other animals. These animals that were eaten were, and are herbivores. These herbivores received their protein from plant based foods. Those carnivorous animals that ate these herbivores received their protein "secondhand". "Those who eat flesh are but eating grains and vegetables at second hand; for the animal receives from these things the nutrition that produces growth. The life that was in the grains and vegetables passes into the eater.

We receive it by eating the flesh of the animal. How much better to get it direct, by eating the food that God provided for our use!"[8] Here we see a principle. Those who eat flesh foods, receive the nutrients (fats, proteins, and etc.) second hand. Most humans and some animals are actually omnivores. Omnivores eat both plant and animal food. So, in these cases some of the nutrients (carbohydrates, proteins, and etc...) are actually first hand while the other is secondhand.

In the body proteins are actually broken down to peptides (amino acids). These amino acids are arranged into specific chains forming specific proteins for different uses in the body. Most people equate protein with meat just like they equate calcium with milk as if these were the only sources. We have already discovered where man, beast, insect, fowl, and etc. receive their protein from "directly" or "indirectly from "plant based foods". Plant based foods are considered by nutritionist to contain incomplete protein. "Such plant-derived foods can nonetheless be excellent sources of protein if eaten in combinations that supply all of the essential amino acids."[9]

Man's diet, as it was originally given contained "variety". It was not a "dog food" diet consisting of "sameness" or a "single item" food. It was God's design to supply man's entire nutrient needs from a variety of foods, not a single item. This diet would sufficiently supply mans needs. The protein when combined from the various foods could also aid in muscular development. "It is a mistake to suppose that muscular strength depends on the use of animal food. The needs of the system can be better supplied, and more vigorous health can be enjoyed, without its use. The grains, with fruits, nuts, and vegetables, contain all the nutritive properties necessary to make good blood. These elements are not so well or so fully supplied by a flesh diet. Had the use of flesh been essential to health and strength, animal food would have been included in the diet appointed man in the beginning."[10] But instead, it came only to meet an emergency, and eventually to satisfy ancient Israel's lust for meats.

PROTEIN CONTENT IN PLANT BASED FOODS[11]

NUT/SEED (1/4 CUP) (SHELLED)	PROTEIN GRAMS	GRAIN 1 CUP (COOKED)	PROTEIN GRAMS
Almond	7	Amaranth	7
Brazil nut	5	Barley, pearled	4 to 5
Cashew	4	Barley, flakes	4
Chestnut	1	Buckwheat groats	5 to 6
Coconut (shredded)	2	Cornmeal (fine grind)	3
Filbert/Hazelnut	5	Cornmeal (polenta, coarse)	3
Flax seed	5	Millet, hulled	8.4
Macadamia	2	Oat Groats	6
Peanut	8	Oat, bran	7
Pecan	2	Quinoa	5
Pine nut	4	Rice, brown	3 to 5
Pistachio	6	Rice, white	4
Pumpkin seed	7	Rice, wild	7
Sesame seed	7	Rye, berries	7
Soy nut	10	Rye, flakes	6
Sunflower seed	8	Spelt, berries	5
Walnut	5	Teff	6
		Triticale	25
		Wheat, whole berries	6 to 9
		Couscous, whole wheat	6
		Wheat, bulgur	5 to 6

VEGETABLE (COOKED)	SERVING	VEGETABLE (COOKED)	SERVING
Artichoke	medium	Kohlrabi	1 cup
Asparagus	5 spears	Leeks	1 cup
Beans, string	1 cup	Lettuce	1 cup
Beets	1/2 cup	Okra	1/2 cup
Broccoli	1/2 cup	Onion	1/2 cup
Brussels Sprouts	1/2 cup	Parsnip	1/2 cup

Cabbage	1/2 cup	Peas	1/2 cup
Carrot	1/2 cup	Peppers, bell	1/2 cup
Cauliflower	1/2 cup	Potato, baked with skin	2 1/3 x 4 3/4"
Celeriac	1 cup	Potato, boiled with skin	1/2 cup
Celery	1 cup	Radish	1 cup
Chard, Swiss	1 cup	Rhubarb	1 cup
Chayote	1 cup	Rutabaga	1 cup
Chives	1 Tbs.	Spinach	1 cup
Collards	1 cup	Squash, Summer	1 cup
Corn, Sweet	1 large cob	Squash, Winter	1 cup
Cucumber	1 cup	Sweet Potato	1 cup
Eggplant	1 cup	Tomato	1 medium
Fennel	1 medium bulb	Turnip	1 cup
Jerusalem Artichoke	1 cup		
Kale	1 cup		

FRUIT (RAW)	SERVING	Honeydew	cup
Apple	2 per lb.	Jackfruit	cup
Apricot	med.	Jujube, dried	1 oz.
Avocado	med.	Kiwi	large
Banana	1	Kumquat	med.
Blackberry	cup	Lemon	1
Blueberry	cup	Lime	1
Boysenberry	cup	Loganberry	cup
Cantaloupe	cup	Loquat	1
Casaba Melon	cup	Mango	1
Cherimoya	1	Mulberry	cup
Cherry	cup	Nectarine	1
Cranberry	cup	Orange	1
Currant	cup	Papaya	cup
Date(pitted)	1/4 cup	Passion fruit	1
Durian	1 cup	Peach	1
Feijoa	med.	Pear	1
Fig	1	Persimmon	1
Gooseberry	cup	Pineapple	cup
Grape	cup	Pineapple	cup
Grapefruit	1/2	Plum	1
Guava	med.	Pomegranate	1

FRUIT (RAW)	SERVING	NUT BUTTERS	
Pomelo	½	Nut/Seed (2 Tb.)	Protein Grams
Prickly Pear	med.		
Quince	med.	Almond	5 to 8
Raspberry	cup	Cashew	4 to 5
Rhubarb	cup	Peanut	7 to 9
Sapote	med.	Sesame Tahini	6
Star Fruit	cup	Soy Nut	6 to 7
Strawberry	cup		
Tangerine	med.	SOY PRODUCTS/PROTEIN GRAMS	SERVING SIZE
		Tofu - Medium to Extra Firm	3 oz.
MILK SUBSTITUTES		Tofu - Soft or Silken	3 oz.
Beverage - 1 cup	Protein Grams	Tempeh	4 oz.
		Textured Vegetable Protein	1/4 cup
Soy Regular	6 to 9		
Soy Low/Nonfat	4		
Rice	1		
Rice and Soy	7		
Oat	4		
Multigrain	5		

Convection ovens allow for even, fast cooking because the temperature stays more consistent, whereas conventional ovens can have pockets of warmer or colder air. Hot air rises, so when cooking food on both racks, dishes on the bottom rack may undercook while the food on top burns, explains Allison Eckelkamp, media representative at General Electric.

A *conventional* oven cooks food by heating the space inside the oven. A *convection* oven cooks food not only by heating the air inside the oven, but also by moving that air around the food. Because a convection oven circulates the hot air, food cooks more quickly and can be cooked at lower temperatures than in a conventional oven.

Most baked recipes are designed for conventional ovens, so if you are cooking the food in a convection oven, you must reduce the time and/or temperature, or else your food will burn. There are three ways to convert conventional oven settings to convection settings, depending on the type of food you are cooking. You can read each method below, or use the convection oven conversion calculator. You can split the difference between methods 1 and 2 by slightly reducing both the time and temperature. A good rule of thumb is to reduce the temperature by 15° - 20° and reduce the time by 10-15%. Use this method for casseroles, potatoes, custards, and baked foods.[12]

WHAT IS "COOKING"?

Cooking is the process of preparing food by using heating mechanisms. Food is any substance consumed to provide nutritional support for the body. It is usually of plant or animal origin, and contains essential nutrients, such as carbohydrates, fats, proteins, vitamins, or minerals. The substance is ingested by an organism and assimilated by the organism's cells in an effort to produce energy, maintain life, and/or stimulate growth. Once again, foods can come from plant or animal foods. But which of the two (plant or animal food) is the "best food". This we will discover shortly. But, let us first take a look at cookery.[13]

HEALTHY COOKERY

One reason why many have become discouraged in practicing health reform is that they have not learned how to cook so that proper food, simply prepared, would supply the place of the diet to which they have been accustomed. They become disgusted with the poorly prepared dishes, and next we hear them say that they have tried the health reform and cannot live in that way. Many attempt to follow out meager instructions in health reform and make such sad work that it results in injury to digestion, and in discouragement to all concerned in the attempt. You profess to be health reformers, and for this very reason you should become good cooks. Those who can avail themselves of the advantages of properly conducted hygienic cooking schools will find it a great benefit both in their own practice and in teaching others.[14]

Often health reform is made health deform by the unpalatable preparation of food. The lack of knowledge regarding healthful cookery must be remedied before health reform is a success.[15]

Greater efforts should be put forth to educate the people in the principles of health reform. More cooking schools should be established, and some should labor from house to house giving instruction in the art of cooking wholesome food. Parents and their children should learn to cook more simply than is usually done. The preparation of so many varied and complex dishes so absorbs the time and attention of many that they are disqualified to teach the truth as it is in Jesus.[16]

As we read the counsel above we learn that there is a way to cook, using simple preparation that would take the place of the diet that many were used to, namely a "flesh diet". We are even given heavenly counsel to establish cooking schools on how to cook wholesome foods. We are told that parents and children should learn to cook more simply. Simple cooking is obviously being contrasted with the way that people were accustomed to cooking. This is the counsel that is given us during the anti-typical Day of Atonement while Christ is ministering in the Most Holy Place. Heavenly counsel employs terms such as "Hygienic Cooking Schools" and, "Healthy Cooking". If there is such a thing as healthy cookery, it then is implied that there is such a thing as poor cookery.

POOR COOKERY

Poor cookery is wearing away the life energies of thousands. More souls are lost from this cause than many realize. In deranges the system and produces disease. In the condition thus induced, heavenly things cannot be readily discerned.[17] {CG 373.4}

Scanty, ill-cooked food depraves the blood by weakening the blood making organs. It deranges the system and brings on disease, with its accompaniment of irritable nerves and bad tempers. The victims of poor cookery are numbered by thousands and tens of thousands. Over many graves might be written: "Died because of poor cooking," "Died of an abused stomach."[18]

Here we find that poor cookery or scanty, ill-cooked food affects our ability to discern heavenly things, produces bad blood by weakening the blood making organs, and the result is death. Notice, the word scanty is used. Scanty means inadequate, meager, or insufficient. Here we find that insufficient food will contribute to the weakening of the blood making organs thus producing depraved blood. Insufficient good food can equate to insufficient elements needed by every cell including the cells of the blood making organs. A diet that is unnecessarily restrictive is forbidden by counsel.

Carefully consider your diet. Study from cause to effect. Cultivate self-control. Keep appetite under the control of reason. Never abuse the stomach by overeating, but do not deprive yourself of the wholesome, palatable food that health demands.[19]

Those who understand the laws of health and who are governed by principle, will shun the extremes, both of indulgence and of restriction. Their diet is chosen, not for the mere gratification of appetite, but for the upbuilding of the body. They seek to preserve every power in the best condition for highest service to God and man. The appetite is under the control of reason and conscience, and they are rewarded with health of body and mind. While they do not urge their views offensively upon others, their example is a testimony in favor of right principles. These persons have a wide influence for good.[20]

ALL NEED TO LEARN HOW TO COOK

Do not neglect to teach your children how to cook. In so doing, you impart to them principles which they must have in their religious education. In giving your children lessons in physiology, and teaching them how to cook with simplicity and yet with skill, you are laying the foundation for the most useful branches of education. Skill is required to make good light bread. There is religion in good cooking, and I question the religion of that class who are too ignorant and too careless to learn to cook.[21]

Men, as well as women, need to understand the simple, healthful preparation of food. Their business often calls them where they cannot obtain wholesome food; then, if they have a knowledge of cookery, they can use it to good purpose.

Both young men and young women should be taught how to cook economically and to dispense with everything in the line of flesh food.[22]

The meals should be varied. The same dishes, prepared in the same way, should not appear on the table meal after meal and day after day. The meals are eaten with greater relish, and the system is better nourished, when the food is varied.

Our bodies are constructed from what we eat; and in order to make tissues of good quality, we must have the right kind of food, and it must be prepared with such skill as will best adapt it to the wants of the system. It is a religious duty for those who cook to learn how to prepare healthful food in a variety of ways, so that it may be both palatable and healthful.[23]

EXTREMES IN THE DIET

The carrying of things to extremes is a matter to be dreaded. It always results in my being compelled to speak to prevent matters from being misunderstood, so that the world will not have cause to think that Seventh-day Adventists are a body of extremists. When we seek to pull people out of the fire on the one hand, the very words which then have to be spoken to correct evils are used to justify indulgence on the other hand. May the Lord keep us from human tests and extremes.

Let no one advance extreme views in regard to what we shall eat and what we shall drink. The Lord has given light. Let our people accept the light and walk in the light. There needs to be a great increase in the knowledge of God and Jesus Christ. This knowledge is eternal life. An increase of piety, of good, humble, spiritual religion would place our people in a position where they could learn of the Great Teacher.

You need not go into the water, or into the fire, but take the middle path, avoiding all extremes. Do not let it appear that you are one-sided, ill-balanced managers. Do not have a meager, poor diet. Do not let any one influence you to have the diet poverty-stricken. Have your food prepared in a healthful, tasteful manner; have your food prepared with a nicety that will correctly represent health reform.

There are many now under the shadow of death who have prepared to do a work for the Master, but who have not felt that a sacred obligation rested upon them to observe the laws of health. The laws of the physical system are indeed the laws of God; but this fact seems to have been forgotten. Some have limited themselves to a diet that cannot sustain them in health. They have not provided nourishing food to take the place of injurious articles; and they have not considered that tact and ingenuity must be exercised in preparing food in the most healthful manner. The system must be properly nourished in order to perform its work. It is contrary to health reform, after cutting off the great variety of unwholesome dishes, to go to the opposite extreme, reducing the quantity and quality of the food to a low standard. Instead of health reform this is health deform.

The great backsliding upon health reform is because unwise minds have handled it and carried it to such extremes that it has disgusted in place of converting people to it. I have been where these radical ideas have been carried out. Vegetables prepared with only water, and everything else in like manner. This kind of cookery is health deform, and there are some minds so constituted that they will accept anything that bears the features of rigorous diet or reform of any kind.

My brethren, I would have you temperate in all things, but be careful that you do not strain the point or run our institution into such a narrow channel that it comes out to a point. You must not fall into every man's notions, but be level-headed, calm, trusting in God.

The people of the world are generally far in the opposite extreme of indulgence and intemperance in eating and drinking; and as the result, lustful practices abound.[24]

The quote above that states, "The Lord has given light. Let our people accept the light and walk in the light." The diet that God advocates for His people during probationary time includes healthy cooked food and sufficient raw food. This diet is composed of fruits, nuts, grains, and vegetables. We have not been given any light to adapt an all raw food diet nor a diet free from vegetables. If God through His instrumentalities did not impart this light (all raw food diet or a diet free from vegetables) I ask a very candid question, who did? No one can come to these conclusions without speculating, twisting scripture, and employing inconsistent principles of interpretations.

From the beginning of the health reform work, we have found it necessary to educate, educate, educate. God desires us to continue this work of educating the people. . . .

In teaching health reform, as in all other gospel work, we are to meet the people where they are. Until we can teach them how to prepare health reform foods that are palatable, nourishing, and yet inexpensive, we are not at liberty to present the most advanced propositions regarding health reform diet.

Let the diet reform be progressive. Let the people be taught how to prepare food without the use of milk or butter. Tell them that the time will soon come when there will be no safety in using eggs, milk, cream, or butter, because disease in animals is increasing in proportion to the increase of wickedness among men. The time is near when, because of the iniquity of the fallen race, the whole animal creation will groan under the diseases that curse our earth.

God will give His people ability and tact to prepare wholesome food without these things. Let our people discard all unwholesome recipes. Let them learn how to live healthfully, teaching to others what they have learned. Let them impart this knowledge as they would Bible instruction. Let them teach the people to preserve the health and increase the strength by avoiding the large amount of cooking that has filled the world with chronic invalids. By precept and example make it plain that the food which God gave Adam in his sinless state is the best for man's use as he seeks to regain that sinless state.[25]

The last sentence is referring to a plant based diet, not a raw food diet. No doubt it probally was raw, but the diet that Adam had before sin was a plant based diet free from animal foods. When this quote is understood in its context, and compared with other quotes it will be seen that counsel is contrasting a plant based diet with a flesh diet. The addition of vegetables did not alter god's design for the human race. Vegetables are of a plant based origin. They came out of the ground. The only thing mentioned as far as food preparation is concerned is the effects of large amounts of cooking. Large amounts, not cooking itself should be avoided. To take the quote above to mean no cooked food would also include dehydrated foods and canning. These are preservative methods that were not needed by Adam. This would also include sprouting. Adam did not need to sprout. He had sufficient elements in the foods given by a His Creator. Further sprouting changes the seeds into an herb. If God wanted man to have herbs in place of seeds, and grains He would have given them permission to eat the herbs of the field. But, it was not needed before sin. Canning, dehydrated foods, and sprouting are fine to eat, but sprouting should not take the place of cooked grains or seeds. The fat content is greater in the seed than in the sprout. Fats are needed for many reasons. Also, the starch in the grain when thoroughly cooked has a greater digestibility than the starch in the sprouts. God gave man the grain, and sprouts should not replace it, but rather serve as and addition to the raw vegetables.

The quote that states, ("Let the diet reform be progressive. Let the people be taught how to prepare food without the use of milk or butter. Tell them that the time will soon come when there will be no safety in using eggs, milk, cream, or butter, because disease in animals is increasing in proportion to the increase of wickedness among men. The time is near when, because of the iniquity of the fallen race, the whole animal creation will groan under the diseases that curse our earth.") speaks of a progressiveness in the transition from a flesh based diet to a flesh based diet. Further, counsel makes this statement. "Among those who are waiting for the coming of the Lord, meat eating will eventually be done away; flesh will cease to form a part of their diet. We should ever keep this end in view, and endeavor to work steadily toward it. I cannot think that in the

49

practice of flesh eating we are in harmony with the light which God has been pleased to give us. All who are connected with our health institutions especially should be educating themselves to subsist on fruits, grains, and vegetables. If we move from principle in these things, if we as Christian reformers educate our own taste, and bring our diet to God's plan, then we may exert an influence upon others in this matter, which will be pleasing to God. [CD 380] A flesh free diet, including its derivatives we should as people should move toward. During this journey our habits of eating and drinking should conform to laws of nature. Beyond this, is adding to GOD'S PLAN.

HOW SHALL WE KNOW WHAT IS THE TRUE DIET

In order to know what are the best foods, we must study God's original plan for man's diet. He who created man and who understands his needs appointed Adam his food. "Behold," He said, "I have given you every herb yielding seed, . . . and every tree, in which is the fruit of a tree yielding seed; to you it shall be for food." Genesis 1:29, A.R.V. Upon leaving Eden to gain his livelihood by tilling the earth under the curse of sin, man received permission to eat also "the herb of the field." Genesis 3:18. [26]

Note we are taken back to Genesis 1:29 and 3:18 to begin our study in determining the best foods for mankind. We are taken to the food articles given at creation in the garden; fruits, nuts, grains, and vegetables!

God gave our first parents the food He designed that the race should eat. It was contrary to His plan to have the life of any creature taken. There was to be no death in Eden. The fruit of the trees in the garden was the food man's wants required. God gave man no permission to eat animal food until after the flood. Everything had been destroyed upon which man could subsist, and therefore the Lord in their necessity gave Noah permission to eat of the clean animals which he had taken with him into the ark. But animal food was not the most healthful article of food for man.

In choosing man's food in Eden, the Lord showed what the best diet was; in the choice made for Israel He taught the same lesson. He brought the Israelites out of Egypt and undertook their training, that they might be a people for His own possession. Through them He desired to bless and teach the world. He provided them with the food best adapted for this purpose, not flesh, but manna, "the bread of heaven." It was only because of their discontent and their murmuring for the fleshpots of Egypt that animal food was granted them, and this only for a short time. Its use brought disease and death to thousands. Yet the restriction to a nonflesh diet was never heartily accepted. It continued to be the cause of discontent and murmuring, open or secret, and it was not made permanent. [27]

You will notice that the lessons taught concerning the best diet in Eden was also taught to Israel through the prophet Moses. God's people like ancient Israel are to look back at Eden and learn the same lesson. That a diet containing flesh foods is not God's will, but rather a plant diet is preferred. Also, Manna was given in place of a flesh food diet. Flesh foods, the killing of an animal, were not in harmony with God's will. Even when He gave the children of Israel the permission to eat flesh foods He did not violate natural law. There were many regulations give to govern its preparation. Christ himself followed this diet, and did not violate natural law. Why, because he obeyed the regulations given to govern the preparation.

LUNCH & ENTRÉE DISHES

BAKED BEANS

4 c. cooked pinto beans
24 oz. tomato sauce
2/3 c. Grandma's molasses
½ c. evaporated cane juice
1 TBSP. onion powder
1 TBSP. garlic powder
¼ tsp. turmeric

½ tsp. Chicken Style Seasoning
1 large diced onion
1 large green pepper
2 tsp. Bakon® Hickory Seasoning
2 T. Bragg's® Liquid Aminos

Sauté onions and green peppers, and then combine all ingredients and bake in a pan for 20 – 30 minutes at 350 degrees.

Variation: Heat the baked beans first before pouring into a pan. Next, using the biscuit recipe, scoop out (ice cream scoop) biscuit mix and put on top of baked beans in columns. Bake until biscuits are done. May sprinkle vegan cheese over the dish. This can be done before or after cooking the dish.

BREAD CRUMB TOPPING

10 slices of bread
1 TBSP. oil
1 ½ tsp. onion powder
1 ½ tsp. paprika

1 tsp. garlic powder
1 tsp. sea salt
¼ c. yeast flakes
½ t. Bakon® Hickory Seasoning

Blend all ingredients in a food processor. This can be sprinkled over casseroles before baking.

BROCCOLI/RICE CHEESE CASSEROLE

2 c. cooked rice
¼ c. green bell peppers diced
¼ c. onions diced

1 ½ c. broccoli florets
sea salt to taste
1x American Cheese Recipe page 64

Bread Crumb Topping Recipe page 52

Sauté onions and bell peppers. Next, mix all ingredients together and bake at 350° for 30 minutes.

BUCKWHEATY

1 c. buckwheat
3 c. water
1 tsp. sea salt
1 tsp. garlic powder
1 TBSP. onion powder

½ tsp. basil
1/8 tsp. celery seed
2 TBSP. more of coconut milk
¼ - ½ c. tomato sauce

Cook buckwheat with water and salt. When the grain is done, add the rest of the ingredients. Let simmer for 20 minutes on low, and then serve.

CALVIN'S FAVORITE BURGER

1 c. bread crumbs
1 c. TVP granules
1 c. water or more
¼ c. gluten flour
¼ c. yeast flakes

2 TBSP. flour
2 TBSP. Beef Style Seasoning
2 TBSP. oil
1 tsp. sweetener
¼ tsp. sesame seed oil

Hydrate the TVP first. Combine the rest of the dry ingredients, and then pour water into the mixture. Form into patties, and then bake for 20-25 minutes. You can be creative with this burger by adding seasonings of your choice.

CANDY YAMS

1 c. water
2 tsp. vanilla flavor
¼ c. cornstarch
1 TBSP. coriander
¼ - ½ c. honey

¼ c. Grandma's molasses or maple syrup
¼ - ½ tsp. sea salt
3 sweet potatoes
1 tsp. cardamom
May add non-hydrogenated butter

Cook all ingredients together except for potatoes, until thickened. Peel and slice yams, then layer them in a pan, and pour the sauce over them. Cover and bake at 350° until tender.

CHEESE BREAD DRESSING

12 slices of toasted bread (lightly buttered)
1x American Cheese Recipe page 64
½ c. boiling soymilk
1 ½ tsp. sage
1 ½ c. green bell peppers diced
1/16-1/8 tsp. cayenne pepper

1 ½ c. red bell peppers
1-½ c. onions chopped
¾ c. diced celery
¼- ½ tsp. sea salt

Cut bread into cubes. Sauté vegetables, and then add seasonings. Mix the rest of the cheese sauce with the mixture of bread. Add more cheese if desired. Bake in a greased baking dish for 40-55 minutes at 350°.

CHEESY COUSCOUS

2 c. couscous	1 c. chopped onions
4 c. water	1 c. chopped green peppers
2-2 ½ tsp. sea salt	1 tsp. sage

1x American Cheese Recipe page 64 (omit celery seed, and add as much cheese as you need)
Boil water first, and then add the couscous and salt to the boiling water. Turn off stove and let sit for 10 minutes. Then mix the cheese with the couscous. Next, sauté onions and pepper, and add to the couscous. Lastly, bake at 350° for 20-30 minutes.

CHICK PEA ALA KING

½ c. raw cashews	4 TBSP. yeast flakes
2 ½ - 3 c. water	2 ½ TBSP. Chicken Style Seasoning
2 TBSP. or more Arrowroot	2 TBSP. garlic powder
2 TBSP. onion powder	1 of 15-oz. can of garbanzo beans
½ tsp. sea salt	1 ½ c. frozen peas
½ tsp. cumin	1 c. diced onions
½ TBSP. basil	½ c. red peppers

Blend first ten ingredients thoroughly. After blending pour into pot and add the rest of the ingredients. Cook on the stove until it is cooked, then turn off the stove. Serve over rice or pasta. May add pimentos to dish.

COOKED VEGETABLES

2 c. water	1 tsp. sea salt
¼- ½ c. coconut milk	2 TBSP. onion powder
1 TBSP. yeast flakes	2 TBSP. garlic powder
1/8 tsp. celery seed	1 c. onions diced
½ tsp. tarragon	¼ c. diced green bell pepper
4 c. vegetables of your choice (peas, mixed veggies, corn etc.)	

Put all ingredients in a pot and cook until done. Serve with your main dish.

CORNFLAKE DRESSING

1x American Cheese Recipe page 64	1 c. bread crumbs
1 large onion	2-4 TBSP. non-hydrogenated oil (optional)
½ c. diced green peppers	4 c. cornflakes (healthy kind, no refined sugars)
½ c. diced celery	

Mix all ingredients together in a bowl except for cheese sauce. Then after mixing them up, add the cheese sauce to the mix. Pour into a greased pan and bake at 350° for 35-45 minutes.

EGGPLANT PARMESAN CASSEROLE

BREADING:
¾ c. whole wheat or unbleached flour
¾ tsp. sea salt
1 TBSP. + ½ tsp. Chicken Style Seasoning
½ tsp. Italian seasoning

¼ c. yeast flakes
1 TBSP. cornmeal
¾ c. bread crumbs

3 medium Eggplants
1 large onion (sliced)

Tomato sauce (your desire)
1x American Cheese Recipe page 64

Combine first seven ingredients in a bowl. Slice up as many eggplants that is needed in ¼ - ½ inch slices. Mix the eggplant with the breading and layer them on a sprayed sheet pan. Cook at 350° for 20 minutes on each side Then, layer tomato sauce, onions, eggplant, cheese sauce, then repeat this process. Lastly sprinkle **1x Parmesan Cheese Recipe on page 65** over the casserole. Bake at 350° for 30- 40 minutes.

EGGPLANT WAFFLES

1 ½ c. rice **or** oat flour
½ c. cornmeal
½ -1 tsp. sea salt
1 TBSP. onion powder
½ tsp. garlic powder

2 TBSP. yeast flakes (optional)
2 c. water
¼ c. coconut
¼ c. almonds
1 c. diced eggplant

Blend thoroughly until smooth. Pour into waffle iron about ¾ -1 cup of the batter. Cook about 10 minutes. Serve **Country Gravy Recipe on page 37** over waffles.

GLAZED BEETS

4 of 14.5-oz. cans of beets
2 TBSP. onion powder
1 tsp. garlic powder
½ c. lemon juice
2/3 c. evaporated cane sugar

2 tsp. Chicken Style Seasoning
¼ c. Arrowroot or cornstarch
½ tsp. basil
½ tsp. sea salt

Mix all together in a pot and cook until thickened.

GLUTEN BURGERS

Burger Ingredients:

1-1 ½ c. water
¾ c. cooked garbanzo beans
½ c. pecans or walnuts
1 c. gluten flour
2 TBSP. whole wheat flour
1 TBSP. Beef Style Seasoning
1 TBSP. sesame seed oil
1 TBSP. onion powder
1 tsp. garlic powder

Broth Ingredients:

5 c. water
5 TBSP. Bragg's® Liquid Aminos
½ t. salt
¼ c. nutritional yeast flakes
1 tsp. Bakon® Hickory Seasoning

Blend all the burger ingredients together, except for the gluten. Next, combine the gluten with the blended ingredients. Cut in shapes of your desire (remember that the gluten slightly swell as a result of the internal steam being trapped creating a leavening effect). Bring broth to a boil first. Then, cook burgers in broth on low for 45 minutes. You may mix small diced onion and or green bell peppers into the burger.

GREEN BEAN & POTATO CASSEROLE

9 c. cubed potatoes (½ x ½ inches)
4 – 6 c. of frozen whole green beans
½ c. oil + ½ tsp. sesame seed oil
¼ c. yeast flakes
2 TBSP. onion powder
1 TBSP. garlic powder

1 TBSP. sea salt
1 tsp. sweetener
2 tsp. Italian seasoning
¼ tsp. cayenne pepper

Mix oil and potatoes together, and then add the rest of the ingredients. Bake in a covered casserole dish for 45 minutes – 1 hour. Afterward, remove covering, and let bake for 15 more minutes.

GREENS

8 lbs. Greens
6 c. tomato juice
1 ¼ c. olive oil
2 TBSP. garlic powder
2 TBSP. onion powder
2 ½ TBSP. sea salt or to taste
1/3 c. Chicken Style Seasoning

1 c. yeast flakes
3 TBSP. lemon juice
2 medium tomatoes, diced
1 c. diced peppers
1 c. diced onions

Pour the tomato juice into a pot, and then add the fresh greens, tomatoes, red peppers, onions and salt. Let greens cook until tender. Next, add remaining ingredients, and cook for 15-20 minutes.

HEARTY SOY BURGER

3 c. TVP granules, grounded
3 c. TVP granules, ungrounded
4 - 5 c. water or more
1 c. gluten flour

½ c. yeast flakes
½ c. oil + ½ tsp. liquid lecithin
6 TBSP. Beef Style Seasoning
1 TBSP. sesame seed oil

Rehydrate the ungrounded TVP, and then combine all the dry ingredients. Next, combine all the wet ingredients, and then add it to the dry mixture. Work the mixture with your hands for 2 minutes, and then let sit until it firms up. Form into patties and bake on a greased sheet pan for about 40 minutes at 350°.

HONEY GLAZED POTATOES

2 medium potatoes cubed
1 medium onion diced
2 cloves garlic minced
2 TBSP. olive oil
2 TBSP. pimentos

¼ c. water
4 TBSP. honey
2 TBSP. Bragg's® Liquid Aminos
½ tsp. salt

1 tsp. sesame seed oil
Pinch of cayenne pepper (optional)

Lightly steam the potatoes in a steamer for 10 minutes. While the potatoes are steaming, sauté the minced garlic and onions in a non-stick skillet. Next, add the potatoes into the skillet, and then add the water, oil, Bragg's®, honey, sesame seed oil, and salt, and let cook on medium heat until thickened. Lastly, add the cayenne pepper, and pimentos, and then bake in the oven for 20 minutes. Do not let the potatoes get to soft.

ITALIAN MEATBALLS 1

4 c. bread crumbs
2 c. cooked brown rice
1 c. grounded pecans
2/3 c. flour
1 large onion diced (small)

3 TBSP. sesame seed oil
1 TBSP. Italian seasoning
2 – 3 tsp. sea salt
¼ tsp. sage

Grind pecans in a blender to make a meal. Next, combine all ingredients together in a bowl, and then form into one inch meatballs. Bake at 350° on a greased cookie sheet for 30 – 40 minutes.

ITALIAN MEATBALLS 2

½ c. pecans (ground)
2 ¼ c. boiling water
1 - 2 tsp. salt
1 tsp. Chicken Style Seasoning
¼ c. yeast flakes
2 ½ tsp. onion powder
1 TBSP. Bakon® Hickory Seasoning

1 TBSP. Italian seasoning
1 ½ tsp. sage
1 TBSP. dill seed
2 ¼ c. oats
2 TBSP. sesame seed oil
1 TBSP. maple syrup

Mix all ingredients together, and let sit for 20 minutes. Then, form into patties of your desired size. Bake on a sprayed pan for 40 minutes at 350° turning over halfway.

MACARONI AND CHEESE 1

8 c. elbow macaroni noodles uncooked
4x American Cheese Sauce page 64, adding 4-8 garlic cloves

or

Cheese Sauce Ingredients:

1 c. cashews
½ c. lemon juice
5 c. water
2 TBSP. sea salt
4 TBSP. onion powder
4 TBSP. garlic powder

3 garlic cloves
2 bay leaves
1 small onion
1 c. pimentos
1 TBSP. honey (optional)
¼ c. cornstarch

First cook the elbow noodles. Cool down noodles by constantly running cold water over them. Blend the rest of the ingredients thoroughly using a portion of the water to blend. Cook blended sauce and remaining water in a sauce pan until thickened. You may need to cut the cheese recipe in half depending on the size of your blender.

Mix noodles with the cheese sauce and bake for 30 minutes at 350° or serve as it is without baking. You may need to add more cheese sauce if you so desire.

MACARONI AND CHEESE 2

1 lb. elbow noodle of choice
1 ½ c. cashews
½ c. lemon juice
3 c. water
2 ½ TBSP. sea salt or as much is desired
2 TBSP. onion powder
2 TBSP. garlic powder

2 garlic cloves
1 TBSP. cornstarch
1 bay leaf
1 c. pimentos
1 TBSP. honey (optional)
½ c. non-hydrogenated butter
½ c. Tofutti® Cream Cheese

First cook the elbow noodles. Cool down noodles by constantly running cold water over them. Blend the rest of the ingredients thoroughly using a portion of the water to blend. Cook blended sauce and remaining water in a sauce pan until thickened. You may need to cut this recipe in half depending on the size of your blender. Mix noodles and remaining ingredients with the cheese sauce and bake for 30 minutes at 350° or serve as it is without baking. You may need to add more cheese sauce if you so desire.

MY FAVORITE MACARONI AND CHEESE

6 c. Elbow noodles
2 c. water
1 c. cashews
½ c. oil
¼ c. pimentos
½ c. yeast flakes
1 TBSP. onion powder

1 TBSP. sweetener
1 TBSP. sea salt (or to taste)
1 tsp. garlic powder
2 TBSP. cornstarch
1 TBSP. soy butter (optional)
1 tsp. lemon juice
½ c. vegan shredded cheese

First cook the elbow noodles. Cool down noodles by constantly running cold water over them. Blend the rest of the ingredients thoroughly using a portion of the water to blend. Cook blended sauce and remaining water in a sauce pan until thickened. You may need to cut the cheese recipe in half depending on the size of your blender. Mix noodles with the cheese sauce and shredded cheese. Then, bake for 30 minutes at 350° in a casserole dish. Make sure to put some shredded cheese on top of the macaroni and cheese, and cover with plastic wrap first, and then with aluminum foil. You may need to add more cheese sauce if you so desire.

MILLET CASSEROLE

2 c. cooked millet
3 TBSP. onion powder
½ TBSP. honey
1 ½ TBSP. garlic powder
1 ½ tsp. sea salt
1 tsp. basil

½ c. olives
1 c. onions diced
½ c. green bell peppers diced
4 c. tomato juice or sauce
½ c. **Pimento Cheese Recipe page 60**

Sauté veggies in water. Then mix all ingredients and bake in a deck pan for 30 minutes at 350°. Serve with garlic bread and peas or of your choice.

OAT BURGERS 1

10 ½ c. rolled oats
2 large onions diced
3 TBSP. fresh grounded cilantro
½ c. red peppers
1 c. walnuts grounded
1 c. pecans grounded
1 TBSP. sweet basil
1 TBSP. Italian seasoning
¼ tsp. sage

2 TBSP. olive oil
2 TBSP. garlic powder
9 c. boiling water
1 c. Bragg's® or 2 -3 TBSP. sea salt
½ c. yeast flakes
2 TBSP. Chicken Style Seasoning
1 TBSP. onion powder

Mix all dry ingredients, and then pour in boiling water, stir and let chill off in refrigerator. Form into patties, bake on a sprayed sheet pan at 350° for 45 minutes turning over half -way.

OAT BURGERS 2

3 ½ c. rolled oats
4 c. boiling water
1 cup TVP granules
1 onion diced
¼ c. - ½ c. grounded flax seeds
1 tsp. Italian seasoning

1 ½ tsp. basil
1 tsp. onion powder
1 tsp. Beef Style Seasoning
½ c. Bragg's® Liquid Aminos
1 c. grounded pecans

Mix all ingredients into a bowl, and let sit in the refrigerator until it firms up. Next, using an ice cream scoop, scoop out onto a cookie sheet pan that has been greased, and then take some wax paper and lay it over the burgers and pat down with a flat object. Another pan may work as well. Bake in the oven at 350° for 40 minutes flipping halfway at 20 minutes. After it is finished, take some vegan sliced cheese and put on top of the burger and cook for about 5 minutes. When done, it may be served as a burger.

OAT BURGERS 3

4 c. rolled oats
4 c. boiling water
½ c. yeast flakes

2 TBSP. Beef Style Seasoning
1 tsp. salt

Pour all the ingredients into the boiling water, and cook on high for 2 minutes stirring constantly. Let sit in the refrigerator until firm. Using an ice cream scoop, form patties and then pat down on a greased pan. Bake for 20 minutes on each side.

ONION CHEESE QUICHE

½ lb. firm tofu, crumbled
½ lb. firm tofu blended (blend with the rest of the next six ingredients)
1 tsp. Chicken Style Seasoning
1 tsp. garlic powder
1 tsp. sesame seed oil
½ tsp. Bakon® Hickory Seasoning (optional)
4 tsp. cornstarch
1 c. water

Sauté:
4 c. sliced onions
1 ½ c. sliced celery
1 c. shredded vegan cheese (mix into the batter at the end)

Crumble ½ lb. tofu into a bowl. Next, blend the next 7 ingredients in a blender, and then combine with the crumbled tofu. Sauté onions and celery, and then add to the mixture along with the cheese. Pour into an uncooked pie crust. Let bake for 45 minutes or until done at 350°.

POTATO SALAD

6 c. potatoes, peeled and cooked (let potatoes chill before mixing)
1 medium onion, chopped
½ c. green peppers
½ c. diced celery
1 c. red peppers
½ tsp. basil

1 tsp. sea salt or to taste
Dash of celery seed
1 TBSP. Chicken Style Seasoning (optional)
2 TBSP. yeast flakes (optional)
1x *Real Mayo Dressing

Mix all ingredients together and chill in the refrigerator. You can add healthy relish. You may purchase kosher dill pickles, ground up into small chunks in a food processor, and add honey and lemon juice.

POTATO PATTIES

4 c. mashed potatoes
1 c. flour
1 TBSP. Featherweight® Baking Powder
½ - ¾ c. yeast flakes
½ c. oil or less

1 ½ tsp. sesame seed oil
1 ½ tsp. sea salt
1 c. diced sautéed onions
1 c. diced sautéed green bell peppers
¼ c. shredded vegan cheese (optional)

Mix all the ingredients in a bowl thoroughly, except for the vegetables and cheese. Next, add the remaining ingredients. Using an ice cream scoop, scoop onto a greased pan and shape into patties. Cook for 30 – 40 minutes turning halfway through the cooking time.

QUINOA BURGERS

2 ½ c. cooked quinoa
¾ c. walnuts
1 tsp. garlic powder
3 TBSP. flour
1 tsp. sea salt to taste
1 chopped onion

¼ c. yeast flakes
¾ c. rolled oats
2 TBSP. onion powder
1 TBSP. Bakon® Hickory Seasoning
1 tsp. sesame seed oil

Mix all ingredients together in a bowl. Form into patties. Bake at 350° for 45 - 55 minutes on sprayed cookie sheet, turning once. Yields one dozen.

SAGE STUFFING

1/3 c. Earth Balance® non-hydrogenated butter
1 c. boiling water
1 ½ tsp. sage
1 tsp. sea salt or as much as desired
¼ tsp. cayenne

4 c. whole wheat bread cubes
½ c. onions
½ c. green bell peppers
½ c. celery

Sauté all veggies, and then pour hot water into the pot. Add the remaining ingredients, ending with the bread. Mix together, and put into greased pan and bake 350° until toasty brown on the top.

SCALLOPED SWEET POTATOES

8 c. peeled and sliced sweet potatoes
½ c. oil (can use a dash of sesame seed oil or coconut oil to enhance the taste)
½ c. sweetener

1 TBSP. coriander
1 tsp. cardamom
½ tsp. salt

Combine together in a bowl. Layer potatoes onto a greased pan. Bake in the oven at 350°. After 20 minutes of cooking, stir every 5 minutes until tender.

SEAFOOD PATTIES

3 c. crumbled tofu
½ c. flour
½ c. yeast flakes
¼ c. oil
1 TBSP. onion powder
½ tsp. garlic powder

2 tsp. Featherweight® Baking Powder
¾ tsp. salt
¼ tsp. sweetener
¼ tsp. sesame seed oil
Pinch of kelp powder

Mix all ingredients together, and form into patties. Bake at 350° for 30 minutes on a greased sheet pan. You may add diced sautéed onions to the patty.

SEASONED TOFU

2 lbs. tofu (frozen then thawed)
Sliced, cubed, or cut into strips

Sprinkle Chicken Style Seasoning, Bakon® Hickory Seasoning, and Italian seasoning. Bake at 350° on a lightly greased pan for 30-45 minutes. Flip if needed. Spread gravy over tofu and bake for 20 minutes.

SIMPLE OAT BURGERS

1 ½ c. hot water
2 TBSP. onion powder
2 ½ c. oats

¼ c. yeast flakes
2 TBSP. olive oil
2 tsp. sea salt

Mix all ingredients with the hot water. Let sit for 15 minutes, then form into patties and bake them on a sheet pan for 35-45 minutes. Turn over half way through cooking.

SIMPLE CANDY YAMS

3 sweet potatoes medium or large
2 TBSP. water
¼ - ½ tsp. coriander
¼ - ½ tsp. cardomon
¼ - ½ tsp. sea salt

¼ c. honey, maple syrup or evaporated cane sugar
3 TBSP. non-hydrogenated butter or as desired (optional)

Slice and peel the yams. Layer in a pan with water, and then sprinkle the coriander, cardamom, salt, and, sweetener over the yams. Next put the batter into the pan, and wrap with first saran wrap, and second aluminum foil. Cook at 350° until sweet potatoes are tender.

SQUASH WAFFLES

1 ½ c. oat meal
½ c. cornmeal
½ tsp. sea salt
1 tsp. onion powder
½ tsp. garlic powder

1 ½ - 2 c. water
¼ c. coconut
1 medium yellow squash
¼ c. sunflower seeds

Blend thoroughly until smooth. Pour into waffle iron about ¾ cup- 1 cup of batter. Cook about 10 minutes. Serve country gravy over waffles. Yields 3 waffles.

SUN BURGER RENEWED

6 c. brown rice (cooked)
1 ½ c. grounded sunflower seeds
1 ½ c. grounded pecans
1 TBSP. garlic powder
1 ½ c. **Sunny Sauce Recipe page 40**

2 TBSP. Chicken Style Seasoning
¼ c. Bragg's® or 1 TBSP. sea salt or more
1 TBSP. honey
2 TBSP. yeast flakes
2 TBSP. flour

Mix all ingredients thoroughly. Form into patties. Cook at 350° for 45 minutes, turning over after 30 minutes. After 45 minutes, spread sun sauce over burgers then cook for 10-15 minutes.

TOFU BURGER

1 TBSP. Chicken Style Seasoning
2 TBSP. onion powder
2 tsp. sea salt
2 ½ TBSP. garlic powder
1 lb. extra firm tofu (mashed thoroughly)
1 ½ tsp. Italian seasoning
½ tsp. sage

1 c. grounded walnut
½ c. breadcrumbs
½ c. yeast flakes
½ c. flour
1 TBSP. olive oil
1 onion chopped

Mix all ingredients together. Add water as needed for binding effect. Form into patties. Put onto a sprayed sheet pan. Bake at 350° for 40 minutes, turning over halfway through cooking.

TOFU RICE CASSEROLE

2 c. brown rice
4 c. water
1 tsp. salt
½ c. coconut milk
2 TBSP. Bragg's® or ½ tsp. salt
2 c. diced onions
2 c. diced red peppers

1 c. corn
1 c. broccoli florets
1 TBSP. olive oil
1 TBSP. onion powder
1 TBSP. garlic powder
1x Scrambled Tofu Recipe page 29

Cook the rice first, and then add the coconut milk and Bragg's®. Sauté the onions, bell peppers, corn, and broccoli in a little water and oil until onions are soft, and then mix with the rice. Add and seasonings last and let cook for 15 minutes.

BASIC INSTRUCTIONS ON PREPARING BEANS

WHY SOAK BEANS?
The skin that surrounds the legume is composed of carbohydrates classified as oligosaccharides, whose molecule is composed of a few units of simple sugars such as galactose. Human beings do not possess the enzymes needed for breaking down these carbohydrates. Nevertheless, the bacteria in the colon, particularly those of the genus Clostridum, are, indeed capable of decomposing them into carbon dioxide, hydrogen, and methane. Foods that Heal By George D. Pamplona-Roger pg. 81

All beans do require relatively long time to cook, however the different types do differ slightly. Here is a chart for various beans and how long they take to cook. Soaking does reduce the cooking times somewhat for all the beans. There are two basic methods for soaking beans:

OVERNIGHT SOAK (LONG TERM):
Simply cover the beans in water and soak them overnight (about 8-10 hours). You don't want to soak the beans for too much longer, then they can absorb too much liquid and loose their texture and flavor. Change the water twice during the soaking process. If however, you soaked your beans and want to wait to cook them, then drain the beans and store in the fridge until you're ready.

QUICK SOAK:
The second method is a little quicker and doesn't require as much preparation. Put the beans in a large pot, add water and bring up to a boil. Let the water boil for about 2 minutes, then remove from the heat, cover the pot and let soak for about 1 hour. Next, pour out the water and replace with more water, only enough to cover the beans.

BEANS-TO-WATER RATIO
All the beans have the same beans-to-water ratio.
- 1 pound of soaked beans need to cook in 4 quarts (16 cups) of water
- 1 pound of unsoaked beans need to cook in 5 quarts (20 cups) of water

COOKING THE BEANS
When cooking the beans, bring the water, the beans and 2 ½ teaspoons of salt to a boil. Reduce the heat and maintain a low simmer during the remainder of the cooking time. (See table 7)

Table 7		
TYPE OF BEANS	**REQUIRED COOKING TIME**	
	Soaked	Unsoaked
Black Beans		
Black-Eyed Peas	1 - 1/4 hours	1 1/2 - 1 3/4 hours
Cannellini Beans	1 - 1 1/4 hours	1 1/2 - 1 3/4 hours
Chickpeas	1 1/2 - 2 hours	2 1/4 - 2 1/2 hours
Great Northern Beans	1 - 1 1/4 hours	1 1/2 - 1 3/4 hours
Navy Beans	1 - 1 1/4 hours	1 1/2 - 1 3/4 hours
Pinto Beans	1 - 1 1/4 hours	1 1/2 - 1 3/4 hours
Red Kidney Beans	1 - 1 1/4 hours	1 1/2 - 1 3/4 hours
Lentils		20 - 30 min

CHEESE

AMERICAN CHEESE

1 c. cashews
1 ¼ c. water
1 TBSP. onion powder
1/3 – ½ c. yeast flakes
½ c. oil (optional)
1 tsp. honey

½ c. lemon juice
1 ½ tsp. sea salt
1 TBSP. garlic powder
4 oz. pimentos
1 bay leaf

Blend thoroughly.

BASIC CHEESE SAUCE

2 c. water
1 c. steamed carrots
½ c. yeast flakes
2 t. sea salt
1 bay leaf
1 TBSP. Bragg's®*
1 TBSP. onion powder

1 TBSP. garlic powder
3 TBSP. cornstarch
½ c. cashews
3 TBSP. lemon juice
2 TBSP. non-hydrogenated butter
1 tsp. Bakon® Hickory Seasoning (optional)

Blend Thoroughly. *If not making macaroni and cheese, omit Bragg's®.

BASIC SOY CHEESE/SPREAD

1 ½ c. water
1 c. oil
½ c. Soy Supreme Powder
1 TBSP. sea salt or less
3 TBSP. onion powder

4 oz. pimentos
1 TBSP. dehydrated and/or grounded red bell peppers
½ tsp. honey
1 tsp. lemon juice

Blend thoroughly. Omit some water to create a spread consistency.

CALVIN'S CHEESE SAUCE

1 ½ c. water
¾ c. cashews
1 c. oil
½ c. pimentos
½ c. yeast flakes
1/3 c. lemon juice

2 – 3 TBSP. sweetener
1 TBSP. salt
2 TBSP. onion powder
1 tsp. garlic powder
Pinch of caraway seed

Blend all ingredients, except for oil and lemon juice. Once blended thoroughly, pour the oil into the blender slowly while it is still blending, and then pour the lemon juice into the blender. It should be thick by this time.

CHEDDAR CHEESE

1 ½ c. water
¾ c. cashews
1 c. oil
½ c. pimentos
½ c. yeast flakes

¼ c. lemon juice
1 TBSP. onion powder
1 tsp. garlic powder
2 tsp. – 1 TBSP. sea salt
Pinch of caraway seed

Blend thoroughly.

CHEESE SAUCE

¼ c. Earth Balance® non-hydrogenated butter
2 TBSP. flour
2 c. soy or almond milk
1 c. nutritional yeast flakes
Pinch of cayenne pepper

1-2 tsp. sea salt (or to taste)
1 tsp. honey
½ tsp. paprika

Blend thoroughly, and then cook until thickened.

NACHO CHEESE

1 c. water
1 c. cashews
½ c. yeast flakes
2 TBSP. fresh lemon juice
½ tsp. cumin
1/8 tsp. cayenne pepper

1 ¼ -1 ½ tsp. sea salt
2 TBSP. onion powder
1 c. pimentos
1 TBSP. garlic powder

Blend all ingredients thoroughly.

PARMESAN CHEESE

1 c. sesame seeds (lightly toasted)
1 ¼ tsp. sea salt
1 TBSP. onion powder
1 TBSP. garlic powder

1/3 c. yeast flakes
1 tsp. basil
¼ tsp. lemon juice

Blend until it is somewhat granulated (do not over blend).

PIMENTO CHEESE

1 c. water
¼ c. nutritional yeast flakes
2 TBSP. raw sesame seeds
½ garlic powder
¼ c. lemon juice
¾ c. raw cashews

1 tsp. sea salt
4 tsp. onion powder
½ c. pimentos
1 TBSP. Bragg's®
2 TBSP. non-hydrogenated butter
Pinch of caraway seed

Place all ingredients in a blender. Blend until smooth and creamy. Drizzle over nacho chips or use to make whole wheat or artichoke macaroni and cheese. Just add to the cooked elbow noodles 2 tablespoons of non-hydrogenated butter and extra salt or to taste.

FATS/LIPIDS

God said, "Behold I have given you every herb bearing seed"... Seeds and Nuts among other things, are considered to be "herb bearing seeds". The highest major nutrient in seeds and nuts is "fat" or "lipids".

Lipids are a broad group of naturally occurring molecules which includes fats, waxes, sterols, fat-soluble vitamins (such as vitamins A, D, E and K), monoglycerides, diglycerides, phospholipids, and others.1

At creation there were essentially five sources of lipids: Plant based foods, Humans, Beasts, Fish, and Fowl. Plant based foods was then the only dietary source of fat for beast, fish and man. Concerning the plant based foods, God said, "to you it shall be for meat". This was law. In fact, plant based foods was the only source of lipids for beasts, fish, and fowl. The lipids in plant based foods describe several molecules existing in the five sources mentioned above. In the bible fats were spoken of in the context of animal, and humans, while oils were spoken of in the context of plant based foods. When solid, they are called "fats" or "butters" and when liquid they are called "oils". 2

FUNCTION OF FATS IN BODY:

* Provides a concentrated energy source.
* Serves as an energy reserve.
* Body has minimal carbohydrate stores, no protein stores, but an almost unlimited capacity to store fat.
* Major component of cell membranes.
* Insulates and protects the body.
* Cushions vital organs/other body parts.
* Keep you warm.
* Stores/transports vitamins/other compounds

Fats and oils are chemical compounds made up hydrogen, oxygen and carbon atoms (CHO)
Three Classes of Fats
Triglycerides
Phospholipids
Sterols

TRIGLYCERIDES

Ninety five percent of the fats in foods are triglycerides. We digest them and break them down into their glycerol backbone and the three fatty acids. We can either use the fatty acids for another purpose (like getting energy) or convert them into triglycerides and store them as body fat.

Two Types of Triglycerides
- Saturated

- Unsaturated

- Saturated fatty acids are filled to capacity with hydrogen atoms.
- Unsaturated fatty acids have places where the carbon bonds are not completely filled with hydrogen atoms.
- Monounsaturated (MUFA) means there is one place where a hydrogen atom is missing.
- Polyunsaturated (PUFA) means 2 or more missing hydrogen atoms.

SATURATED FATS

Characteristics of Saturated Fats
- Straight in shape has no double bonds
- No electrical charge
- High smoke
- Solid at room temperature
- Generally from animal sources (exceptions are tropical oils)

Saturated Fatty Acids (Sa FAs) are found in all food fats and oils, but are especially abundant in hard fats. An excess of SaFAs can cause health problems for our heart and arteries.3 We need saturated fat as well as unsaturated fat. Saturated fats make the cell membrane hard and unsaturated fatty acids make the membrane more fluid. It is cholesterol that actually regulates these two fatty acids. Some saturated fatty acids are long, some are medium, and some are short. It is the short and medium chain fatty acids that are used by the body for energy. The long chain fatty acids in foods are actually stored as body fat (short or medium chain fatty acids).

UNSATURATED FATS

- Monounsaturated

- Polyunsaturated

CHARACTERISTICS OF HIGHLY MONOUNSATURATED FATS
> Oils are liquid at room temp
> Not used in deep fat frying-burn too easily
> Examples: olive oil, avocados (little or no G. I. values in oils, nuts, and meats)

CHARACTERISTICS OF HIGHLY POLYUNSATURATED FATS
> oils that burn at low temps
> liquid at room temperature
> breaks down or becomes rancid easily when exposed to heat, light or air. (refrigeration will slow rancidity)
> Plant based fats are mostly mono & polyunsaturated (tropical oils our an exception)

THE EXTRACTING AND REFINING OF OIL

EXTRACTING INVOLVES ESSENTIALLY ONE OF THREE PROCESSES:
- Cold pressed – seeds are pressed against a press called cold pressing. These oils are usually unrefined and are sold as specialty oils. These normally retain the full flavor of the plant from which it was extracted.
- Expeller-pressed – seeds are normally squeezed at high temperatures to generate more oil. These oils normally retain their flavor, color, aroma, and nutrients.
- Chemical solvents – oils are normally extracted using chemical solvents. This is the case with most chemical solvents
-

REFINING INVOLVES ESSENTIALLY FIVE STEPS:
- Degumming – water combined with the oil forms gums. While adding hot water and spinning at high speeds the gums are finally removed.
- Neutralizing – free fatty acids are removed by adding an alkaline medium to change the fatty acid to an insoluble soap.

- Washing/Drying – soap are removed by washing the oil with water. The water id drained, and the oil is dried .under a vacuum
- Bleaching - soap is removed by adding absorbent materials. The absorbent color matter is then filtered out.
- Deodorizing – steam passes through the oil to remove volatile compounds that cause off odors.3

Refined Oils contain no vitamins, minerals, fiber or other natural protection; hence they are calorie dense, nutritionally deficient, and turn rancid quickly when exposed to heat, light or air. Buy oils in a colored container or cover it with a colored bag. Store in the refrigerator or in a cooler place. Refined oils are preferred in high heat cooking. Being free from many substances, they have a higher heating point, almost neutral flavor & aroma, clearer color, and a longer shelf life. Refined oils are in reality designed for high heating cooking such as frying or deep frying. I do not recommend frying at all. The recipes contained in this book use oil to make sauces, creams, desserts, low & high baking, and sautéing. However, unrefined oils are healthier and even preffered over refined oils. The best unrefined oils to use for cooking can be procured from the internet.

You can use unrefined oils for sautéing, low heat cooking (under 300? - mostly 250º). For high heat baking use refined oil (sparingly) or unrefined oils that can remain relatively fine under heating. Most of your sauces do not need to be heated; therefore, you can use unrefined oils in the recipes requiring sautéing and low heat baking. If olive oil is used, use virgin olive oil (this is unrefined) particularly for baked goods. Be aware that olive oil can somewhat change the taste of the baked good. This is only a potential concern with sweet pastries.

SOUPS

GARBANZO SOUP

15 oz. cooked garbanzo beans
1 large diced onion
½ c. zucchini, diced
2 ½ c. water
2 TBSP. yeast flakes
¼ c. coconut milk

3 TBSP. onion powder
1 tsp. garlic powder
2-3 TBSP. flour
1 tsp. sea salt
1 c. chopped cabbage or squash

Cook all, except for flour. When it is hot, add flour and stir until thicken. Serve over rice, biscuits, noodles or savory waffles.

GOLDEN BARLEY STEW

2 c. barley or rice
4 c. water

1 tsp. sea salt

Cook for 45-60 minutes.

SAUCE:
½ c. cashews
½ c. flour
2 c. water

½ c. Chicken Style Seasoning
¼ tsp. celery seed
¼ tsp. marjoram

Blend all these ingredients thoroughly.

1 c. peas
1 c. lima beans

1 c. black eye peas
1 c. carrots

Mix the cashew blend together with the barley and add 2-3 c water. Add the peas, beans, and carrots. Taste and see if it has enough salt that you desire. Serve with crackers, cornbread, or garlic bread.

KATIE'S COCONUT-BEAN SOUP

2 bay leaves
3 garlic cloves
1 ½ c. chopped onions
2 garlic cloves minced
½ tsp. cardamom
1 medium bell pepper chopped
2 medium tomatoes
1 tsp. sea salt or to taste

1 TBSP. maple syrup
3 TBSP. fresh lemon juice
1 ½ c. coconut milk
½ c. cooked rice
1 c. dried navy beans, soaked in vegetable stock
½ tsp. of turmeric, onion powder, garlic salt, and cumin

Cook beans in vegetable stock (enough to cover about 1") with bay leaves and whole garlic cloves (discard when beans are done). While beans are cooking, sauté onions, minced garlic and spices until translucent, then add peppers, tomatoes, maple syrup, and lemon juice and simmer until tender. Stir in coconut milk and rice. When beans are tender, add everything together, you may need to add more stock. You can garnish with toasted coconut.

LENTIL SOUP

6 c. lentils (uncooked)
14 c. water
2-3 TBSP. onion powder
2-3 TBSP. garlic powder
4 bay leaves
2 potatoes, diced
5 carrots, sliced
2 bell peppers, diced

1 onion diced
¾ c. yeast flakes
2 tsp. basil
½ tsp. fennel seeds
1 can coconut milk
2 TBSP. sea salt
1x American Cheese Recipe page 64

Cook lentils until tender, then add all the other ingredients, except for potatoes and carrots. Steam carrots and potatoes until tender, then add to the rest of soup. Lastly, add the cheese sauce and let simmer for 10 minutes.

SUGAR

Sugar is universally known for its "sweet" taste. Sugar is a "carbohydrate", which is the most abundant nutrient in the original diet, next to water. Glucose is a sugar that is needed by the body for fuel. Especially is this the case with the brain, and nervous system. Glucose is a free and single sugar. Therefore, the body does need free sugar. But, how much, and at what rate? What sources? Does the bible talk about free sugars?

All sweeteners and substitute sweeteners come from plant based sources with exception of lactose, which comes from animal. Some are perhaps natural or synthetically made. The wisest man that ever lived second to Christ, was Solomon. His wisdom under the inspiration of the Holy Ghost was expressed in three books in the bible, Proverbs, Song of Solomon, and Ecclesiastes. In the book of proverbs he says, "My son, eat thou honey, because it is good; and the honeycomb, [which is] sweet to thy taste:"[71] Solomon gives the two reasons why we could eat it. He says, "because it is good", and "because it is sweet to thy taste". "Our tongues have four basic types of taste buds: bitter, sour, salty, and sweet."[72]

God created these buds. After sin, through indulgence, these taste buds became perverted. If you like sweets, that is ok. God gave you the taste bud. However, if our taste buds guide us in the selection of foods, this can be dangerous. Humans are a higher creature, and must therefore consider what sweets, and how much is good for proper physiology and anatomy. A nineteen-century author said, "Carefully consider your diet. Study from cause to effect. Cultivate self-control. Keep appetite under the control of reason. Never abuse the stomach by overeating, but do not deprive yourself of the wholesome, palatable food that health demands."[73] Good counsel! We should take time to consider what we are putting into this "intelligent design", and study from cause to effect. Appetite, including her servants (e.g., taste, hear, and etc...) are to be subject to the higher powers of the mind.

Since the Bible specifically identifies honey as being good, we want to find out why it is good, and why is it sweet. Let us first describe the processing of honey. Bees suck nectar, a sweet sugary substance produced by flowers and other open parts of plants. In the stomach of a bee this sweet substance is mixed with water and enzymes. These enzymes digest disaccharides (two sugars joined together) called saccharose into two monosaccharides (single sugars) called glucose and fructose. The sugars are then regurgitated, and then passed onto other bees to continue the process of predigestion (3-4 times). This predigested substance called honey is placed in cells in the honeycomb for preservation.

Honey is composed of 17-20% water (after it dries in the honeycomb), 80-82% carbohydrates (31% glucose & 38% fructose). It also contains proteins, minerals, vitamins, organic acids, enzymes, substances that antibacterial, and etc. It is also sweet due to its fructose content. Honey is composed of single sugars and therefore do not require digestion as most other sugars. This takes a load off of the stomach and pancreas. In the digestion of white sugar, calcium and B-vitamins are needed. Therefore, the body uses its reserves to assist in the digestion of carbohydrates found in white sugar.

Sugars in the fruits are the best. Next would be dried fruits since they still contain fiber, minerals and vitamins. Next would be molasses because of its high mineral content, and B-vitamins. However, honey must be remembered for its overall benefits on the body. Raw Honey would probably be next, then maple syrup. Lastly, turbinado or evaporated cane sugars are acceptable. White sugar is not even considered. On just about any food pyramid, you will notice that free sugar, along with desserts are not given any serving Recommendations, but rather that if it is used, it should be used sparingly. The wise man Solomon said "It is not good to eat much honey... eat so much as is sufficient for thee, lest thou be filled therewith, and vomit it."[74] Therefore, use the above sweeteners moderately, and in most cases, sparingly.

DESSERTS

APPLE PIE

6-8 apples peeled and slice (Granny Smith & Gala)
1 container apple juice concentrate
pinch of salt
3 tsp. cornstarch

1 ½ tsp. coriander
½ tsp. cardamon
3 TBSP. non-hydrogenated butter

Put all ingredients into a pot, and then add two containers of cold water to the pot. Stir and cook until thickened. Put into an uncooked pie shell dish, and cover with another layer of **Whole Wheat Pastry Pie Crust on page 80**. Pinch the edges and the poke a few holes in the top of the pie. Bake in the oven for 35 minutes at 350° or until done.

BANANA PUDDING

4 TBSP. cornstarch
2 c. soy milk
¼ c. soy powder
4 TBSP. non-hydrogenated butter

2 ½ tsp. vanilla flavor
1-2 tsp. banana flavor
½ c. evaporated cane sugar or honey
1 banana (omit if using a different flavor)

Blend all the ingredients together. Then cook on the stove until thickened. Let cool in the refrigerator. After cooled down, blend with a hand mixer.
Variations: May use blueberries, or different flavorings such as vanilla, lemon, banana, etc.

BASIC CAKE DRY MIX

1 c. unbleached flour
1 c. whole wheat flour
1 TBSP. Featherweight® Baking Powder
1 tsp. sea salt

¾ c. evaporated cane sugar
1 tsp. cornstarch

Sift dry ingredients together 3 times, store in refrigerator or freezer until needed.

CAKE ICING

1 TBSP. vanilla flavor
Pinch of sea salt
½ tsp. almond flavor (optional)
1-8 oz. Tofutti® Non-Dairy Cream Cheese

¼ c. - ½ c. powdered fructose or evaporated cane sugar (or to taste and consistency)
1/3 c. Earth Balance® or Soy Garden® non-hydrogenated butter

Mix in a bow with a mixer until smooth, and then store in refrigerator until ready to use.

CALVIN'S CAKE

1 ½ c. unbleached flour
½ c. whole wheat pastry
½ - ¾ c. evaporated cane juice
¾ tsp. sea salt
¼ c. oil

¼ c. non hydrogenated butter
1 TBSP. cornstarch
1 TBSP. Featherweight® Baking Powder
1 ½ TBSP. vanilla flavor
¾ -1 c. soy milk or pineapple juice

Mix all the dry ingredients, except Featherweight®, together in a bowl with a hand mixture for 2 minutes. Next, cut the oil into the dry ingredients, and then pour the liquid into the dry ingredients until cake batter consistency. Next, fold vanilla flavor and feather weight into the batter and pour into a greased and floured cake pan. Bake for 35-45 minutes at 350° in the oven.

CALVIN'S CAKE ICING

¼ c. coconut milk
1 c. water
½ c. lecithin granules
12 oz. silken tofu
2 tsp. sea salt

1 TBSP. vanilla flavor
1 tsp. almond flavor or lemon flavor
½ c. coconut oil (organic expeller press)
½ c. soybean or safflower oil (expeller press)
¾ c. powdered evaporated cane juice

Blend all ingredients thoroughly, and let sit until firm in the refrigerator.

CAROB CAKE

1x Basic Cake Dry Mix page 74
1 tsp. Roma® Coffee Substitute
1 c. water

¼ tsp. maple flavoring
¼ - ½ c. carob powder (before adding the liquid)

Mix the dry ingredients with the **Basic Cake Dry Mix**, and add the liquid ingredients, then blend for 2 minutes. Bake at 350° for 35 minutes in a greased and floured cake pan.

CAROB CUPCAKES

1 1/2 c. whole wheat pastry
1/4 c. carob powder
1 TBSP. Featherweight® Baking Powder
3/4 c. evaporated cane sugar
2 TBSP. Roma® Coffee Substitute
½ tsp. salt

1 TBSP. lemon juice
1 TBSP. vanilla
½ c. oil
½ tsp. liquid lecithin
1 c. water

Preheat oven to 350°. Grease or spray an 8x8 inch pan. Combine wet ingredients in bowl. Combine dry ingredients and sift over wet mixture and stir enough to distribute all ingredients. Pour into greased pan and bake at 350° for 25-30 minutes. Remove from oven and cool. Prepare frosting by mixing sugar, carob, and soy milk in a sauce pan. Heat to boiling and boil for 3 minutes, stirring occasionally. Cool. Beat the powdered sugar and vanilla into cool mixture. Frost the cooled cake.

CALVIN'S CAROB CHIP COOKIES

2/3 – ¾ c. evaporated cane sugar
1 ½ TBSP. vanilla flavor
¾ tsp. sea salt
½ c. carob chips
¼ c. shredded coconut

½ c. whole wheat flour (pastry)
1 ½ c. unbleached flour
3 tsp. Featherweight® Baking Powder
½ c. oil
½ tsp. butter flavoring

¼ - ½ c. ice cold water or soy milk, just enough to give it a cookie dough consistency

Cut the oil into the flour, salt, baking powder, and sugar. Next, add the carob chips, and coconut. Afterward, add the liquid and flavorings, and then roll out into ½ - 1-inch balls, place on a sprayed cookie sheet, and then press down. Make sure that there is some space in between the cookies. Bake at 350° for 12-15 minutes until lightly brown at bottom of cookie.

CAROB BROWNIES

½ c. non-hydrogenated butter
1 c. carob chips
½ c. cane sugar
½ c. maple syrup
2 TBSP. soy milk
1 c. whole wheat pastry flour

½ c. unbleached flour
1 - 2 TBSP. vanilla flavor
1 TBSP. +1 tsp. Featherweight® Baking Powder
1 tsp. sea salt
1 c. chopped almonds
1 c. creamy almond butter

In a sauce pan, melt the first five ingredients until smooth. Pour into a bowl with the remaining ingredients and mix well. Bake in a pan at 350° for about 35 – 40 minutes. To check if it is done, you may stick a tooth pick. If the toothpick comes out clean when you pull it out and the brownies pull away from the sides of pan, the brownies are ready. The batter will rise and fall. You can sprinkle carob chips on the top.

CAROB CHIP COOKIES

½ c. maple syrup or honey
1TBSP. vanilla flavor
¾ tsp. sea salt
½ c. oil
¼ - ½ c. soy milk
½ tsp. Grandma's molasses

1 ½ c. unbleached flour
½ c. pecans
1 t. Featherweight® Baking Powder
½ c. carob chips
1 ½ c. whole wheat flour or pastry flour

Mix all the dry ingredients. Blend all the wet ingredients. Combine together. Using a ½ cup, measure out 12 cookies, place on a oil sprayed cookie sheet bake at 350° for 25 - 35 minutes.

CAROB FROSTING

2 c. carob chips
1 c. hot soymilk
½ c. Better Than Ice Cream® Powder

1 TBSP. vanilla flavor
¼ c. coconut milk
1 tsp. cornstarch

Blend thoroughly in a blender until smooth.

COCONUT CAKE

1 ½ c. unbleached flour
½ c. whole wheat pastry flour
¾ tsp. sea salt
1 TBSP. Featherweight® Baking Powder
¾ c. evaporated cane sugar

½ c. oil
½ - ¾ c. soy milk
¼ c. shredded coconut
1 ½ TBSP. vanilla flavor
¾ c. coconut milk

Combine all dry ingredients in a bowl, and then mix oil into the dry mixture. Pour the rest of the liquid into the bowl and blend for 2 minutes. Pour into a cake pan greased and floured, and bake at 350° for 35 minutes. To check if the cake is done, you may stick a toothpick in the middle of the cake, and when you pull the toothpick out and it comes out clean, then it is done. You can add a teaspoon of gluten flour or more to give the cake a sponge cake texture.

GLAZE

½ c. soy butter, whipped
1 tsp. cornstarch
1 tsp. vanilla flavor (oil based preferred)

Powdered cane juice sugar as much is needed
Pinch of salt
Soymilk according to desired consistency

Using a mixing bowl, mix in first the whipped butter, vanilla flavor, salt, cornstarch, powdered sugar, and the soymilk. Add just enough soymilk to obtain desired consistency.

HONEY TOPPING

1/3 c. flour
1 c. maple syrup
1/3 c. oil or non-hydrogenated butter
¼ tsp. coriander + cardamom
1 TBSP. vanilla flavor

1 c. chopped pecans
¼ tsp. sea salt
¼ tsp. Featherweight® Baking Powder

Mix together in a bowl. Sprinkle over a cake before it is cooked.

HONEY PECAN CAKE

1 c. wheat flour
1 c. unbleached flour
1 tsp. sea salt
3 tsp. Energy® or Featherweight® Baking Powder
1 tsp. egg replacer
1 tsp. lecithin oil

1 c. soy milk
1 ½ - 2 TBSP. vanilla flavor
½ c. coconut milk
¼ tsp. lemon flavor (optional)
½ - 1 c. evaporated cane sugar
1/3 c. oil or non-hydrogenated butter

Sift flour, salt and feather weight. Preheat oven to 375*. Mix flour mixture, sweetener, and egg replacer together. Mix the oil and the lecithin oil together and add to the mixture. Add soymilk and flavoring then blend for 2 minutes. Pour into greased 8" pan. Add the *Honey Topping recipe on top and spread over the cake. Bake for 35 – 45 minutes.

LEMON COOKIES

¾ - 1 c. evaporated cane sugar
1 TBSP. vanilla flavor
½ - 1 TBSP. lemon flavor
¾ -1 tsp. sea salt
¼ c. pineapple juice
½ c. whole wheat pastry flour
1 ½ c. unbleached flour

½ c. chopped pecans
¾ c. oil or non hydrogenated butter
1 TBSP. Energy® or Featherweight® Baking Powder

Blend first 7 ingredients, and then mix last ingredients. Next, measure out ½ cup of dough and place on a cookie sheet. Sprinkle evaporated cane juice over the top of the cookies. Bake at 350°for 15- 25 minutes or until slightly brown on the bottom.

LEMON SPICE CAKE

1 ½ c. unbleached flour
½ c. whole wheat flour
¾ tsp. sea salt
1 ½ tsp. coriander
1 ½ tsp. cardamom
1 tsp. egg replacer
1 tsp. cornstarch
¾ c. - 1 c. evaporated cane sugar

½ c. oil
1 c. water
1 TBSP. lemon flavor
2 TBSP. vanilla flavor
3 TBSP. Grandma's molasses
1 TBSP. Featherweight® Baking Powder

Mix all ingredients together thoroughly, except for Featherweight®. Then, mix Featherweight® with the cake batter. Pour into a greased pan and cook at 375° for 35-45 minutes. When done, take it out of the oven and let cool.

LEMON SPICE MUFFINS

1 c. whole wheat pastry flour
1 c. unbleached flour
2/3 c. evaporate cane juice
½ tsp. lemon rind
1/3- ½ c. oil
1 c. soy milk

1 TBSP. coriander
1 tsp. cardamom
½ tsp. anise
1 T. Featherweight® Baking Powder

Mix the dry ingredients together in a bowl. Next, cut the oil into the mixture and then add the rest of the ingredients. Afterwards, pour into a greased and floured pan and bake at 350° for 25 minutes.

MAMA G'S SPICE CAKE

4 c. sifted unbleached flour
4 t. Featherweight® Baking Powder
1 rounded tsp. sea salt
¼ tsp. cardamom
1 ½ tsp. vanilla flavor

¼ tsp. coriander
1 c. oil non-hydrogenated butter
1 c. succanat (cane sugar)
1 c. Grandma's molasses

Sift flour 3 times, adding the salt, Featherweight®, and the spices on the last sift. Blend the liquids together thoroughly, and combine with the dry ingredients. Using a hand mixer, whip the batter for 2 minutes. Spray or grease a cake pan and pour the batter into the pan. Bake at 350° for 35 minutes or check the middle of the cake with a knife or fork, if nothing comes out, then pull out of the oven and let cool.

OATMEAL RAISIN COOKIES

2 c. quick oats
2/3 c. flour
2/3 c. evaporated cane juice
½ tsp. sea salt
½ c. oil or non-hydrogenated butter
2 – 4 TBSP. soy milk
1 TBSP. vanilla flavor
½ tsp. Grandma's molasses
2 tsp. coriander

1 tsp. cardamom
¼ tsp. anise
½ tsp. Featherweight® Baking Powder
½ c. raisins
¼ c. shredded coconut
½ c. pecans
2 TBSP. grounded flaxseed

Combine all ingredients. Make into ¼ cup size pieces and place on a greased cookie sheet. Cook for 20 – 30 minutes at 350°.

OIL-LESS COOKIES

2 c. walnuts (grounded)
½ c. sesame seeds
1 ½ c. whole wheat pastry flour
¾ c. maple syrup

1 T. vanilla flavor
¼ c. shredded coconut
½ t. sea salt

Mix all ingredients into a bowl thoroughly. Next, shape into cookies and place onto a cookie sheet. Bake at 350º for 15 – 20 minutes.

ORANGE PINEAPPLE PIE

1 c. unsweetened pineapple juice
1 c. fresh squeezed orange juice
Dash of salt
1 tsp. orange rind

¼ tsp. lemon flavor
1/3 c. cornstarch
½ c. honey
½ tsp. vanilla flavor

Mix together in a bowl and then thicken on the stove. Next, put into a precooked pie crust dish. You may put soy whip cream on top of the pie, and then refrigerate.

PLAIN CAKE

1x **Basic Cake Dry Mix Recipe page 74**
2 TBSP. vanilla flavor
1 tsp. Energy® Egg Replacer

1/3 c. oil
1 c. soy milk

With a hand mixture, mix all ingredients in a bowl for 2 minutes. Bake at 350° for 35 – 45 minutes.

SPICE CAKE 1

1x **Basic Cake Dry Mix Recipe page 74**
¾ tsp. coriander
½ tsp. cardamom
¼ tsp. anise
1/3 c. oil
2 TBSP. Blackstrap molasses

1 TBSP. coconut milk
1 ½-1 TBSP. vanilla flavor
1 c. water

Mix the dry ingredients with **the Basic Cake Dry Mix Recipe**, and add the liquid, then mix for 2 minutes with a hand mixture. Bake at 350° for 35 – 40 minutes.

SPICE CAKE 2

1 ½ c. unbleached flour
½ c. whole wheat pastry flour
2 tsp. coriander
2 tsp. cardamom
1 tsp. anise
2 TBSP. cornstarch
¾ tsp. sea salt
1 T. Featherweight® Baking Powder

½ c. oil
1 TBSP. vanilla flavor
½ c. Blackstrap molasses
½ c. succanat or evaporated cane sugar
½ -1 c. soy milk (more or less until cake consistency is reached)

In a bowl, sift the dry ingredients twice. In another bowl, mix thoroughly the liquid ingredients (start out first with ½ cup soymilk and add as needed). Combine dry and liquid, and then blend with a hand mixture for 2 minutes. Pour mixture into a greased and floured pan, and bake at 350° for 35 - 45 minutes or until done.

SWEET POTATO PIE

6 c. cooked carrots or sweet potatoes cooked until soft
¼ t. salt
1/3 c. earth balance
2 t. lemon flavor

2 T vanilla flavor
1/3 c. arrowroot or cornstarch
1 c. evaporated cane sugar (more or less)
1x Wheat Crust Recipe

Blend sweet potatoes and carrots in a blender or food processor. Next, mix all ingredients until creamy pour onto the semi-baked pie crust. Cook for about 20 minutes at 350°.

TOASTED SPICE CAKE

1 ½ c. whole wheat pastry flour (toasted)
½ c. unbleached flour
½ c. evaporated cane juice, or succanat
1 tsp. coriander
1 tsp. cardamom
1 tsp. sea salt
¾ -1 c. soy milk or as needed (cake consistency)

¼ c. Grandma's molasses
1/3 c. oil or non hydrogenated butter
1 TBSP. Featherweight® Baking Powder
2 TBSP. vanilla flavor
1 TBSP. orange rind

Mix the dry ingredients, except for Featherweight® in a bowl, and add the liquid ingredients, then blend for 2 minutes. Afterward, put Featherweight® in the bowl, and blend for an additional 10 – 15 seconds. Pour into a cake pan and bake at 350° for 35 - 45 minutes.

VANILLA COOKIES

½ - ¾ c. evaporated cane sugar
¾ tsp. sea salt
1 ½ c. unbleached flour
½ c. whole wheat pastry flour
1 TBSP. Featherweight® Baking Powder
2 TBSP. vanilla flavor

½ c. soy milk or just enough to give it a cookie dough consistency
½ c. oil

Mix or combine first 6 ingredients. Mix the rest of the ingredients. Combine them both, and then measure out 1/8 cup size cookies, placed on a sprayed cookie sheet. Bake at 350° for 15- 20 minutes until slightly brown. For variations, add shredded coconut and sprinkle a mixture of evaporated cane juice, coriander, and cardamom.

VANILLA PUDDING 1

½ c. evaporated cane sugar
2-3 TBSP. cornstarch
2 c. soy milk
¼ c. Better Than Ice Cream® Powder

2-3 TBSP. non-hydrogenated butter or oil
1 TBSP. vanilla flavor
¼ tsp. cardamom

¼ tsp. of coriander (omit coriander and cardamom if making banana pudding)

Blend all ingredients up thoroughly, and then cook on the stove until thicken. Let chill in the refrigerator.

VANILLA PUDDING 2

¼ c. oil
½ c. evaporated cane juice
1/8 tsp. sea salt
1 ½ TBSP. vanilla flavor
½ lb. silken tofu

1 tsp. lecithin granules
1/3 c. Vanilla Better Than Ice Cream®
2 TBSP. non-hydrogenated butter
¾ c. soy milk

Blend all ingredients up thoroughly, and then let chill in the refrigerator.

BREADS

BANANA BREAD

1 ½ c. unbleached flour
½ c. whole wheat flour
½ - ¾ c. evaporated cane sugar
¾ tsp. sea salt
1 TBSP. Featherweight® Baking Powder
½ c. oil or non-hydrogenated butter
3 – 4 TBSP. Grandma's molasses

1 c. chopped walnuts
½ tsp. cornstarch
3 TBSP. soy milk or as needed
1 TBSP. vanilla flavor
3 ripe bananas

Combine all the dry ingredients and sift twice, except for Featherweight®. Mix all the liquid ingredients together, including bananas, for 1 minute, and then combine the liquid with the dry ingredients. Mix for 1 minute, and then fold Featherweight® into the batter. Pour into a floured and greased pan, and bake at 375° for 35-45 minutes until done.

BISCUITS

1 c. soy milk (more or less)
½ c. oil
1 ½ tsp. sea salt
1 ½ c. unbleached flour
½ c. whole wheat flour

1 TBSP. Energy® or Featherweight® Baking Powder
1 ½ TBSP. honey
1 ½ TBSP. yeast flakes

Sift salt and flour together. Mix oil + lecithin and honey together, and then mix into flour. Mix Featherweight® and yeast flakes in the mix. Then, mix soymilk until the dough is moist. Drop biscuits onto a sprayed pan. Bake at 400° until golden brown at the bottom.

CALVIN'S FAVORITE CORNBREAD

1 ½ c. cornmeal
½ c. unbleached flour
1 TBSP. Featherweight® Baking Powder
1 tsp. sea salt
¼ - ½ c. evaporated cane sugar or honey

½ c. oil
1 c. warm soy milk or water
1 TBSP. vanilla flavor (for cornbread cake)

Mix all dry ingredients, except Featherweight®, then combine the wet ingredients, and thoroughly mix together. Next, fold Featherweight® in, and then in a pan or muffin pan bake at 350° for 30-35 minutes.

CORNBREAD - SPELT

1 ½ c. cornmeal
½ c. spelt flour
1 TBSP. Featherweight® Baking Powder

½ - 1 tsp. sea salt
¼ - ½ c. xylitol (sugar substitute, excellent for diabetics)

½ c. golden grounded flaxseeds
1 ½ - 2 c. water

1 TBSP. lecithin granules
1 TBSP. vanilla flavor (for cornbread cake)

Mix all dry ingredients, except Featherweight®, then combine the wet ingredients, and thoroughly mix together. Next, fold Featherweight® in, and then in a pan or muffin pan bake at 350° for 30-35 minutes.

CORNBREAD

3 c. cornmeal
2 c. whole wheat or unbleached flour
2 tsp. sea salt
4 tsp. Featherweight® Baking Powder

2-2 ½ c. soy milk or water
2/3 c. oil
2 TBSP. evaporated cane sugar

Mix all dry ingredients together. Mix all wet ingredients together. Then combine together. Pour into a sprayed pan or muffin pan and bake at 350° for 40 minutes or until browned on edges.
Note: If you use honey use less water.

DINNER ROLLS

2 tsp. dry yeast
1 c. warm water
2 TBSP. honey
1 tsp. sea salt
1 ½ tsp. onion powder
1 ½ tsp. garlic powder

2 TBSP. yeast flakes
1 tsp. egg replacer
3 TBSP. oil or non-hydrogenated butter
2 TBSP. gluten flour (must be mixed with the remaining flour)
2¼ c. flour

Dissolve yeast in warm water in large mixer bowl. Add honey, salt, egg replacer, oil, and 1 c. of flour. Beat until smooth. Stir in seasonings, gluten, and remaining flour; continue beating until smooth. Scrape batter from side of the bowl. Cover; let rise in warm place until double, about ½ hour. Stir down batter and spoon into greased muffin pans. Let rise until double, about 30 minutes. Heat oven to 400° and bake about 15-25 minutes.

GARDEN CRACKERS

1 c. whole wheat flour
1 c. unbleached flour
½ c. oil
½ c. soy milk
1 TBSP. onion powder

2 TBSP. garlic powder
¼ c. yeast flakes
1 ½ tsp. sea salt
2 t. basil

Combine all dry ingredients. Blend all liquids. Combine them together and form into dough. Roll out onto a sheet pan about 1/8 – ¼ inch thick. Cook at 350° for 35-45 minutes, or until slightly browned on the bottom.

KATIE'S WHOLE WHEAT BREAD

6 c. warm yeast water with temperature of 110°
4 ½ T. yeast
¾ c. honey
2 T. sea salt
6 c. whole wheat flour

2-3 T. gluten flour
¼ c. soy flour
2 T. liquid lecithin
10-12 c. additional flour

Combine water, yeast (room temperature), and honey. Mix and allow to sit for 5 minutes until it foams. Add 6 cups of flour, salt, gluten and soy flour, and lecithin. Mix on medium speed or by hand until flour is moistened, then mix for an additional 3 minutes or 5 minutes by hands to work gluten well. Let rise for 8 minutes. It should get much bigger. Add the last 10-12 cups of flour a little bit at a time with the machine on low until it begins to hold together and pull away from the side of the bowl (hand method) or mix until too stiff to stir, and transfer onto floured surface and knead in additional flour. Be careful not add too much! The dough should be slightly sticky, but if you pinch of a little bit and roll it between your fingers it should not stick. Knead in machine on medium-low speed for 8 – 15 minutes or about 10 minutes. By hand, fold the dough and push with the palm of your hand. Knead by hand into 6 ½ pound loaves. Cover with light towel and let rise for about 30 minutes in an 80-85° environment allowing to double in size. Bake at 375° for 10 minutes. Watch out for burning on the bottom rack. Remove from pans, and oil tops, then let cool on racks.

PIZZA CRUST

4 c. flour
1 ¼ warm water
1 tsp. active dry yeast
2 TBSP. olive oil

1 tsp. salt
2 tsp. honey
2 tsp. yeast flakes

Sift flour and salt into a large bowl. Combine water, yeast, honey, olive oil, and yeast flakes in a bowl, and gradually pour into the flour mixture. Mix into a dough. Knead on a lightly floured surface for about 10 minutes, until dough is smooth, springy, and elastic. Place dough in a greased and floured bowl, cover and let rise in a warm place for 1 - 1 ½ hours. When dough is ready, preheat the oven to 425°. Brush four baking sheets with oil. Knead the dough for 2 minutes, then divide into four equal pieces. Roll out each to a 10-inch round, stretching, and piecing any uneven or torn pieces of dough. Place onto a baking sheet. Bake for 15 minutes or until golden brown AFTER you have put your desired toppings on the pizza dough. See **Pizza Toppings** and **Pizza Sauce Recipes** on pages 38, 39.

SPELT BISCUITS

2 c. spelt flour
½ c. grounded flaxseeds
1-2 TBSP. lecithin granules
½ tsp. sea salt

1/3 c. xylitol
2 c. water or more
1 TBSP. Featherweight® Baking Powder

Mix thoroughly. Use an ice cream scoop to drop onto a greased pan. Cook biscuits for 30-40 minutes at 350°. Brush soy or coconut oil over the biscuits.

WHEAT CRUST

1 c. whole wheat pastry flour
1 c. unbleached flour
½ c. cold soy milk

1 tsp. sea salt
½ c. oil + 2 TBSP. soft non-hydrogenated butter

Combine all the dry ingredients, and then blend all wet ingredients in a blender. Combine wet and dry ingredients together. Roll out on a sheet pan or in a pie dish that you plan to use. You can also roll out onto wax paper. Bake for 30 minutes at 350°.

WHOLE WHEAT BROWN BREAD

3 c. whole wheat flour
1 c. unbleached white flour
1/3 c. non hydrogenated butter
1 t. sea salt
1 T. Featherweight® Baking Powder

¼ c. honey
1 oz. soymilk
(pour in a bit at a time until the dough is moist)

Preheat the oven to 425°. Lightly grease and flour a cake pan. In a large bowl, sift and combine all the dry ingredients. Rub in the butter until the flour is crumbly. Add the soymilk to form a sticky dough. Place on floured surface and lightly knead. Shape into a round flat shape in a round cake pan and cut a cross in the top of the dough. Cover the pan with another pan and bake for 30 minutes. Remove cover and bake for an additional 15 minutes.

WHOLE WHEAT PASTRY PIE CRUST

1/3 c. non hydrogenated butter
4 TBSP. soy milk

1 c. whole wheat pastry flour
1 tsp. sea salt

Cut the butter into the salt and flour, and then pour water into the mixture. You may not need all of the water. Form into a ball and roll out on a flour sheet of wax paper. Next, put it into a pie dish and bake at 350° or until lightly brown.

INGREDIENTS SUBSTITUTE GUIDELINE

The Ingredient Substitute Guideline (ISG) was developed for the express purpose of minimizing the need for more cookbooks focusing on particular diseases, and to make it easier for persons with special health needs to be able to apply certain guidelines to most cookbooks.

To assist those who have willed to live healthier in using almost any cookbook to accommodate their specific health needs, and to minimize discouragement, and labor is our goal. Our higher goal is to aid persons in their character development by engendering and encouraging healthy eating producing a healthy body and ultimately a healthy mind.

SUGARS:

FRUCTOSE: 1/2 cup fructose = 1 cup white sugar.

MAPLE SYRUP: 3/4 cup maple syrup for 1 cup white sugar. Reduce liquid in recipe by 3 tablespoons.

MAPLE SUGAR: 1 cup maple sugar = 1 cup white sugar.

BARLEY MALT SYRUP: Substitute 1 1/3 cups barley malt for 1 cup white sugar. Reduce liquid in recipe by 1/4 cup. Purchase only 100% barley malt, not barley/corn malt syrup. It has a strong flavor and is usually used in combination with other sugars such as molasses in foods like gingerbread, baked beans, and bread.

BROWN RICE SYRUP: Substitute 1 1/3 cups for 1 cup white sugar. Reduce liquid by 1/4 cup per cup of rice syrup. In baking, rice syrup is most often combined with maple syrup.

CONCENTRATED FRUIT JUICE: Substitute 2/3 cup concentrate for 1 cup white sugar. Reduce liquid by 1/3 cup per cup fruit concentrate. Reduce oven 25 degrees and adjust Baking Time for a Slightly Longer Period.

DATE SUGAR: Substitute 1 cup for 1 cup white sugar. Add hot water to dissolve date sugar before using in batters. Use it in combination with other sweeteners such as maple syrup or honey. Lower baking temp 25 degrees and adjust baking time for a longer period.

SUCANAT: Use 1 cup sucanat per 1 cup white sugar. Add 1/4 teaspoon baking soda per cup dried cane juice.

HONEY: Substituting honey for sugar seems to be a matter of taste. Some people use it cup for cup, others prefer 1/2 cup – 2/3 cup of honey per cup of white sugar. Reduce the amount of other liquids by 1/4 cup for every cup of honey used. Lower the oven temp about 25 degrees F to prevent over-browning.[1]
In baked products, no more than half the granulated sugar should be replaced with honey. Use 1 part honey for every 1 ¼ parts sugar. Reduce the liquid in the recipe by ¼ cup because honey is largely water.[2]

SUGAR ALTERNATIVES

STEVIA, XYLITOL, and **AGAVE** are less processed than refined sugar and still have their nutrients intact, which allows the body to absorb and use the other nutrients that your body needs. Although they have calories like refined sugar, they are more slowly metabolized by the body.[3]

STEVIA:
- Here is a Stevia conversion chart:
- 1 Tsp Stevia (powered) =1 Cup Sugar

- 1 Tsp Stevia (liquid)=1 Cup Sugar
- 1/2 Tsp Stevia=1 Tbsp Sugar
- 6 Drops liquid Stevia=1 Tbsp Sugar
- A pinch of Stevia=1 Tsp sugar
- 2 drops liquid Stevia=1 Tsp sugar4

THESE ARE APPROXIMATE MEASUREMENTS DUE TO MANY FACTORS SUCH AS:
- Sour Ingredients
- Personal Preference
- Cultural Differences
- Manufacturing Company

XYLITOL: 1 cup of Xylitol = 1 cup of white sugar

Xylitol is sugar alcohol. Though similar to ethyl alcohol, it does not exert the same influence upon the central nervous system as ethyl alcohol and does not produce any drunkenness symptoms. It is derived from the fibers of various berries, and other fruits. However, most of the Xylitol sold in the health food stores are not from fruits, but rather from fibers within the corn cob. Xylitol should be eaten in moderation. Excessive consumption can result in flatulence, and diarrhea. Most people do not have any problems. Anything over 40 grams (per day) is excessive.

AGAVE: Substitute 2/3 cup agave nectar per 1 cup sugar.

Compensate for the moisture in the agave nectar by reducing other liquids added by 1 fl oz per 2/3 cup agave used. Or, estimate the moisture to be approx. 20% of the agave used. If the recipe calls for no liquid, add 3-5 Tbs. (22.5 – 37.5g) of flour for each ¾ cup (180 ml) of liquid sweetener. To avoid over browning, oven temperature should be reduced by 25 deg. F and baking time increased by 6% to compensate. 5

SALT

GRANULATED SALT:

Common Salt is composed primarily of sodium chloride, with 60% chlorine and 40% sodium.6 Sodium is essential to the body. It is one of the main components that compose extracellular fluid that surrounds the cells. It is needed to maintain constant fluid symmetry and arterial pressure.

Sea salt is similar to common salt with the exception of its small amounts of the salts of calcium, potassium, magnesium. Refined seal salt lacks the magnesium and calcium.

The salt normally used in most homes and restaurants (refined table salt) is very different from unrefined Sea Salt. Table salts are mined from the earth with bulldozers and heavy machinery, and then iodized, bleached, and diluted with anti-caking agents. Chemicals are added to refined salt in the processing and all the beneficial minerals and trace elements that are found in natural Celtic Sea Salt are removed.7

Celtic Salt is one of the best salts to use because of its additional minerals. The additional minerals compensate for some of the harmful affects of excess sodium.

¾ t. -1 Tbs. of Celtic sea salt is equivalent to approximately 1 Tbs. of common salt.

SOY SAUCE SUBSTITUTE

LIQUID BRAGGS AMINO

It is a soy sauce substitute. One cup of LBA is equivalent to one cup of soy sauce.

SOY SAUCE SUBSTITUTE
- 4 tablespoons beef style seasoning
- 4 teaspoons lemon juice
- 2 teaspoons dark molasses
- 1/4 teaspoon ground ginger
- 1 pinch cayenne pepper
- 1 pinch garlic powder
- 1 1/2 cups water

In a saucepan over medium heat, stir together the beef style seasoning, lemon juice, molasses, ginger, cayenne pepper, garlic powder and water. Boil gently until liquid is reduced to about 1 cup, about 15 minutes. Add Celtic salt to taste.

LIQUID BRAGGS AMINOS

Bragg Liquid Aminos is a Certified NON-GMO liquid protein concentrate, derived from soybeans, that contains the following Essential and Non-essential Amino Acids in naturally occurring amounts.8 However, it should be used in moderation and in some cases sparingly.

STARCHES/THICKENERS

WHEAT FLOUR (ALL-PURPOSE)
- -Poor resistance to thinning when overcooked.
- -Fair gel formation.

CORNSTARCH
- -Good resistance to thinning when overcooked.
- -Good gel formation.
- -Does not freeze well.

ARROWROOT
- -Good resistance to thinning when overcooked.
- -Fair gel formation.
- -Does not reheat well.

TAPIOCA
- -Fair - Poor resistance to thinning when overcooked.
- -Poor gel formation.
- -Freezes well.

POTATO STARCH
- -Fair resistance to thinning when overcooked.
- -Poor gel formation

RICE FLOUR

- -Good resistance to thinning when overcooked.
- -Poor gel formation.
- -Freezes well.

SUBSTITUTION FOR THICKENERS

For every 2 T. of flour, substitute:
- 4 T. browned flour
- 1 T. cornstarch
- 2-1/2 t. arrowroot
- 1 T. tapioca (quick cooking, granulated)
- 1 T. potato starch
- 2-1/2 t. rice flour or rice starch

Note: 3 t = 1 T

Use arrowroot in place of cornstarch. It has a lower glycemic index than cornstarch. Excess starch is stored as fat in the body. This raises the triglyceride levels in the body, increase weight, and burdens the pancreas. You may want to consider using Agar-Agar. However, it does not freeze well. Arrowroot is clearer than cornstarch, but cornstarch firms up better. DO NOT OVERCOOK ARROWROOT! It will loose its consistency.

ARROWROOT AS A THICKENER

The word arrowroot is believed to originate with Native Americans, who used the root to draw out poison from arrow wounds. Another possible origin is a Native American word for flour, Araruta. Its scientific name is Maranta arundinacea.

We couldn't ask for a better thickener. This silky white powder is a pure starch derived from a tropical American plant. It is fat-free, easy to digest and flavorless (so it won't interfere with the delicate sauces). It thickens at low temperature and is perfect for heat-sensitive egg-based sauces and custards. It has twice the thickening power of wheat flour and does not get cloudy upon thickening, so it makes beautiful fruit sauces and gravies. Moreover it has none of the chalky taste associated with cornstarch.

To store arrowroot, keep in an airtight container marked with the date that you bought it. It's best to use within 2 months because its thickening properties diminish with age. When using arrowroot, dissolve 1 1/2 teaspoons arrowroot in 1 tablespoon cold liquid. Stir or whisk the cold mixture into 1 cup of hot liquid at the end of the cooking time. Stir until thickened which is about 5 seconds. These proportions will make about 1 cup of medium-thick sauce, soup or gravy. For thinner sauce, use 1 teaspoon arrowroot. For a thicker sauce, use up to 1 tablespoon arrowroot.

If you are using it to replace cornstarch, use 1 tablespoon arrowroot in place of 2 teaspoons cornstarch. When replacing flour use half as much arrowroot as flour. If the recipe calls for 1 tablespoon flour, substitute with 1½ teaspoons arrowroot. To keep an arrowroot-thickened sauce thick, just stir until just combined. Over-stirring can make it thin again.9

XANTHAN GUM

A common food additive used as a thickener in salad dressings and other processed food products. According to Bob's Red Mill, it is made from a tiny microorganism called Xanthomonas campestris and is a natural carbohydrate. The gum can be used to making breads and baked products for people with allergies to gluten. It should be noted that some people report allergies to this gum product so those people should read food labels carefully.10

AGAR AGAR

What is Agar Agar? "This natural additive is prepared from several species of red algae. It is a vegetable gelatin, one with high gelling properties, and used by vegetarians because true gelatin is made from calf's feet.

Agar forms a gel at 88° F and does not melt below 136°F. It is unflavored and is rich in iodine and trace minerals. Agar's setting properties are stronger than unflavored gelatin and will set at room temperature after an hour. It is a high protein food and should be refrigerated for storage.

Agar's gelling ability is affected by high acidity. More acidic foods like strawberries and citrus may require a higher agar to liquid ratio...The basic Agar Gel recipe is 2 teaspoons of powder to 2 cups of liquid. Soak the agar in the liquid for about 10-15 min. Bring to boil and simmer stirring until the agar completely dissolves (about 5 minutes).11 It is a good substitute for gelatin. 1 tsp. of Agar Agar powder is equivalent to 1 Tbs. of Gelatin.

COCOA SUBSTITUTE

CAROB POWDER/FLOUR

Carob powder is made from the toasted, then ground, pods of the Carob tree. Carob is used as a substitute for chocolate although totally different substance. To substitute carob powder for cocoa, replace one part cocoa with one and one-half to two parts carob by weight.12

CASHEWS SUBSTITUTE

Almonds can be used in place of cashews. Boil 2 cups of water, and then put the same amount of almonds as you would nuts into the boiling water. Let boil for 1 minute, afterward strain the water of the almonds. Cool the almonds down in cold water. Next, proceed in taking of the skin of the almond. The Glycemic index of almonds and basically all nuts is rounded off to "0"'. Use equal amounts in any recipe that calls cashews.

WHEAT FLOUR SUBSTITUTE

There is nothing that can substitute for wheat flour perfectly, however, spelt flour, can be used as a replacement.

GLUTEN FREE FLOUR

King Arthur Flour is the name brand of a gluten free multipurpose flour. It is wheat free, soy free, and nut free. The ingredients are: rice flour, tapioca starch, potato starch, and whole grain brown rice flour.

MISCELLANEOUS SUBSTITUTES

- Feather Weight (Hains): Baking powder substitute
- Egg Replacer (Energy): Is made from potato starch (main ingredient)
- Coriander and Cardamom: Cinnamon and nutmeg substitute
- 1 Tb of Coriander powder
- 1 tsp of Cardamom powder
- ¼ tsp of Anise powder
- Yeast Flakes: Gives food a cheesy flavor
- Bakon Seasoning: Gives a hickory style flavor
- Carob Chips: Non-Dairy substitute for chocolate (Non-hydrogenated)

- Breading Base: This is to cover foods such as tofu slices before putting the breading flour on it.

BLEND TOGETHER THE FOLLOWING:

- 1 c. egg replacer
- 1 c. oil
- 2 c. water
- ¼ c. chicken style seasoning
- 1 T. sesame seed oil

THESE ITEMS CAN BE PURCHASED AT MOST HEALTH FOOD STORES.

Blend Tec Blender – Most of the recipes requiring blending was developed with the Blend Tec Blender. This Blender is a recommended investment in order to obtain the best results. For more information please contact M.E.E.T. Ministry at 1-731-986-3518. I would encourage you to develop a saving plan for the Blend Tec. Believe me, it's worth it!

Harmful beverages are usually non-nutritive. This would include: coffee, tea, soda, and alcoholic beverages.

Let us talk about stimulating beverages.

CAFFEINE

Caffeine is a stimulant and not a thirst quencher. It is added to a number of beverages. Chocolate contains a central nervous system stimulant very similar in structure to caffeine, called theobromine. "Caffeine is a toxic alkaloid belonging to the purine chemical group."[1] Purine is uric acid producing. Uric acid as well as other acids that result form metabolism are excreted by the kidneys. The kidneys need water in order to excrete these acids constantly and efficiently. This is done by selective cells that reabsorb bases so as to maintain the proper PH Caffeine must be eliminated due to the body's inability to store it.

It is called a central nervous system stimulant because of its ability to enter nerve cells stimulating the transmission of nervous impulses between the nerve cells. This can lead to false energy called "stimulation", and not actual energy as is produced through oxidation of carbohydrates. "The disease related to caffeine intake involves every organ system, from the nervous system to the skin. Caffeine raises stress hormone levels in the blood, inhibits important enzyme systems having to do with house cleaning in the body, sensitizes nerve reception sites, and is associated with a sense of poor health, anxiety, and depression.[2, 3]

EFFECTS OF CAFFEINE:

- Stimulate the nervous system
- Alter mood and behavior
- Produce a stress reaction
- Pour out adrenaline into the system

- Constrict blood vessels
- Increase blood pressure
- Increase pulse
- Increase stomach acid

CAFFEINE AND THE FRONTAL LOBE

According to a figure found in the book "Proof Positive" by Neil Nedley, two out of the eight ways caffeine affects the brain are:
- May influence the risk of other diseases that in turn exert frontal lobe effects through physical or mental stress.
- May exert effects that impact on spiritual and social dimensions of our character.

Anything that affects our frontal lobe directly or indirectly is a fleshly lust that war against our spiritual nature. Our frontal lobe need to as far as possible be preserved so that we may be able to reason, and choose spiritual things.

Caffeine is not the only concern when it comes to roasted coffee. There are other negative effects of coffee not caused by caffeine but rather by other substances that are in both coffee, and decaffeinated coffee. There are literally hundreds of dangerous materials. "The effects on caffeine on children are more intense than on adults; nervous excitation, hyperactivity, behavioral problems, and sleep disorders.[4] Tea is less harmful than coffee since it contains less caffeine and does contain two types of medically active phytochemicals. However, a broad study in Great Britain shows that those drinking more than 8 cups of tea a day are 2.4 times more likely to die from a heart attack or a stroke.[5] Tea contains substances that destroys vitamin B_1.[6]

TEA AND COFFEE ARE CONTRIBUTING FACTORS.

"Through the intemperance begun at home, the digestive organs first become weakened, and soon ordinary food does not satisfy the appetite. Unhealthy conditions are established, and there is a craving for more stimulating food. Tea and coffee produce an immediate effect. Under the influence of these poisons the nervous system is excited; and in some cases, for the time being, the intellect seems to be invigorated, the imagination more vivid. Because these stimulants produce such agreeable results, many conclude that they really need them; but there is always a reaction. The nervous system has borrowed power from its future resources for present use, and all this temporary invigoration is followed by a corresponding depression. The suddenness of the relief obtained from tea and coffee is an evidence that what seems to be strength is only nervous excitement, and consequently must be an injury to the system."[7]

What power can the tobacco devotee have to stay the progress of intemperance? There must be a revolution upon the subject of tobacco before the ax will be laid at the root of the tree. Tea, coffee, and tobacco, as well as alcoholic drinks, are different degrees in the scale of artificial stimulants. The effect of tea and coffee, as heretofore shown, tends in the same direction as that of wine and cider, liquor and tobacco.

Tea is a stimulant, and to a certain extent produces intoxication. It gradually impairs the energy of body and mind. Its first effect is exhilarating, because it quickens the motions of the living machinery; and the tea-drinker thinks that it is doing him great service. But this is a mistake. When its influence is gone, the unnatural force abates, and the result is languor and debility corresponding to the artificial vivacity imparted. The second effect of tea drinking is headache, wakefulness, palpitation of the heart, indigestion, trembling, and many other evils.

Coffee is a hurtful indulgence. It temporarily excites the mind to unwonted action, but the after-effect is exhaustion, prostration, paralysis of the mental, moral, and physical powers. The mind becomes enervated, and unless through determined effort the habit is overcome, the activity of the brain is permanently lessened. All these nerve irritants are wearing away the life-forces, and the restlessness caused by shattered nerves, the impatience, the mental feebleness, become a warring element, antagonizing to spiritual progress. Then should not those who advocate temperance and reform be awake to counteract the evils of these injurious drinks?[8]

ALCOHOL

In the beginning God created food from the earth for man to subsist upon. Man's original diet was composed of essentially four food groups (fruits, nuts, grains and vegetables) concerning this diet God said "it was good". The adversary of man and God had no power to create, but He could pervert that which God created. He first corrupted the nature of man, the crowning act of creation. Every other created thing was afterward corrupted. Satan has taken foods from each one of these groups, and has converted them to poisonous concoctions. " Satan gathered the fallen angels together to devise some way of doing the most possible evil to the human family. **One proposition after another was made, till finally Satan himself thought of a plan. He would take the fruit of the vine, also wheat, and other things given by God as food, and would convert them into poisons, which would ruin man's physical, mental, and moral powers, and so**

overcome the senses that Satan should have full control. Under the influence of liquor, men would be led to commit crimes of all kinds. Through perverted appetite the world would be made corrupt. By leading men to drink alcohol, Satan would cause them to descend lower and lower in the scale."[9] With this in mind, why is alcohol legalized? It makes one wonder who is behind this nonsense!!! It is none other than Satan.

Another word for alcohol is "ethanol". "The ethanol may be derived from many different sources including wine, cider, beer or fermented fruit juice, or it may be made synthetically from natural gas and petroleum derivatives.[10] Satan can essentially (through human instruments) make alcohol from fruit (grapes, apples, bananas, and etc.), grains (wheat, rice, barley, and etc...), nuts (coconut...), and other sources. It is the carbohydrate in the foods, for the most part that is converted to alcohol through a fermentation process. Alcohol is formed when yeast enzymes break up sugar into roughly the same parts of alcohol and carbon dioxide gas.

"Alcohol is the favorite mood-altering drug in the United States and its effects, both pleasant and unpleasant, are well-known. What may not be well known is the fact that alcohol is a toxic drug that produces pathological changes (cirrhosis) in liver tissue and can cause death.[11]

Alcohol is readily absorbed from the gastrointestinal tract; however, alcohol cannot be stored and therefore, the body must oxidize it to get rid of it. Alcohol can only be oxidized in the liver, where enzymes are found to initiate process.

The first step in the metabolism of alcohol is the oxidation of ethanol to acetaldehyde catalyzed by alcohol/dehydrogenase containing the coenzyme NAD^+. The acetaldehyde is further oxidized to acetic acid and finally CO_2 and water through the citric acid cycle. A number of metabolic effects from alcohol are directly linked to the production of an excess of both NADH and acetaldehyde."[12] But what many do not know is that alcohol can be converted to vinegar.

ALCOHOL   **VINEGAR**

 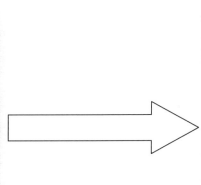 

WHAT IS VINEGAR?

The word "vinegar" derives from the Old French, *vin aigre*, meaning "sour wine".[13] It is acetic acid that gives vinegar its sour taste. There are different sources of vinegar in the bible. In the book of numbers we find this text, "He shall separate [himself] from wine and strong drink, and shall drink no **vinegar of wine**, or **vinegar of strong drink**, neither shall he drink any liquor of grapes, nor eat moist grapes, or dried."[14] There are other sources. You will notice that wine is a vinegar source. What is it in wine that fosters the development of vinegar. "It has been known from antiquity that wine sours when it is left open to the air. This way "vinum acrus"- sour wine" – vinegar was obtained, but without knowing why. In 1846 Pasteur discovered that a bacteria called "mycodermia aceti" ferments wine, transforming its **alcohol** into **acetic acid**. Any alcoholic beverage can be used to make vinegar."

Just as there are enzymes in the liver that initiates the process of the oxidation of alcohol, so also is this the case with acetic acid. "An enzyme capable of decomposing aceto-acetic acid without acetone formation was found to be present in normal liver tissue."[5] "Alcohol is one of the toxins that the liver doesn't handle as well as others. The liver cannot regenerate after being damaged by alcohol. ...Alcohol prevents the release of glucose from the liver and can cause low blood sugar."[16] It [alcohol] puts a burden on the liver which does not function normally while processing alcohol. "One of the livers function is to manufacture 800-1500 milligrams of cholesterol per day..."[17] While the body is busy processing alcohol, acetaldehyde, acetic acid and finally into CO_2 & water, it does not release glucose from the liver, nor manufacture normal amounts of cholesterol, and it doesn't process fats, and proteins efficiently. This is probably why those who drink vinegar daily experience lower, cholesterol and blood sugar levels, and weight loss. But note, this does not address the cause, but rather mask the problem.

VINEGAR IN THE BIBLE

Jesus said, "They gave me also gall for my meat; and in my thirst they gave me vinegar to drink"[18], and Matthew also records the fulfillment of this verse, "They gave him vinegar to drink mingled with gall (bitter poisonous substance): and when he had tasted [thereof], he would not drink"[19]. ".... The Saviour declared, "Reproach hath broken My heart; and I am full of heaviness: and I looked for some to take pity, but there was none; and for comforters, but I found none. They gave Me also gall for My meat; and in My thirst they gave Me vinegar to drink." Psalm 69:20, 21. To those who suffered death by the cross, it was permitted to give a stupefying potion, to deaden the sense of pain. This was offered to Jesus; but when He had tasted it, He refused it. He would receive nothing that could becloud His mind. His faith must keep fast hold upon God. This was His only strength. To becloud His senses would give Satan an advantage."[20]

VINEGAR & THE TEETH

The Wise Man Solomon said "as vinegar to the teeth, and as smoke to the eyes, so [is] the sluggard to them that send him."[21] What does vinegar do to the teeth? The acid in vinegar when it comes in contact with the enamel of the teeth which is essentially calcium (calcium is alkaline) it erodes the enamel.

VINEGAR & DIGESTION OF CARBOHYDRATES

The digestive juice in the mouth is alkaline. When vinegar comes in contact with the digestive juice it has the ability to deactivate the enzymes thus hindering the digestion of carbohydrates. The body cannot utilize any major nutrients unless they are broken down to a smaller substance. In this case it is carbohydrates. This perhaps is the reason why it is recommended for weight lost. But this comes with some consequences. Though excess carbohydrates may not be desired, it is nonetheless the cleanest source of energy, and is used especially by the brain cells at a much rapid pace than in other cells in the body. When there is an imbalance between the major nutrients (carbohydrates, protein, and fats) particularly when the carbohydrate daily percentage drops low, the body has to use proteins, and fats for energy. This can impact both the kidney and liver significantly. In conclusion, I do not recommend vinegar in the diet. However, there may be foods that contain an extremely minimal amount that in my estimation will probably not do any harm. But remember, lemon juice is better.

POP

One of the main sources of hidden sugar is soft drinks or soda pop. Soft drinks were unknown until modern times. However, in 1994 the average American consumed 52.2 gallons of soft drinks, with 40 gallons of it in the form of regular (non- diet) beverages.[22] A12 fl oz. soda pop among a variety of brands (all brands not included) contain 125-189 calories from sugar. This would be equivalent to 8-12 ¼ tsp. of sugar.[22]

COOKBOOK RECIPES INDEX

REFERENCES

MAN'S FIRST CLASS ON NUTRITION/FIRST SECTION

1. King James Version, Genesis 1:29
2. King James Version, Genesis 2:16, 17
3. King James Version, 1 John 3:4
4. King James Version, Ephesians 2:8, 9
5. King James Version, Romans 3:22
6. King James Version, James 2:26
7. King James Version, Isaiah 43:7
8. King James Version, Amos 3:7
9. King James Version, Revelation 12:17
10. King James Version, Revelation 19:10
11. King James Version, Genesis 1:11
12. King James Version, Genesis 3:22, 24
13. King James Version, Genesis 3:19
14. King James Version, Genesis 22:14
15. King James Version, Thessalonians 4:16
16. King James Version, 1 Corinthians 15:51-55
17. Whitney, Ellie & Rolfes, Sharon R. *Understanding Nutrition*, 10th Edition, p. 1.
18. King James Version, Genesis 1:2, 9, 10
19. King James Version, Genesis 2:10
20. Greenhalgh, Alison (March 2001). "Healthy living - Water". *BBC Health*. Retrieved 2011-02-19.
21. King James Version, Genesis 3:19
22. The Gemini Geek, Geek Redefined – Why do People Sweat – viewed 2011-2-19.
23. King James Version, Genesis 3:21
24. The Gemini Geek, Geek Redefined – Why do People Sweat – viewed 2011-2-19.
25. Ibid.
26. Whitney, Ellie & Rolfes, Sharon R. *Understanding Nutrition*, 10th Edition, p. 397.
27. King James Version, Genesis 3:19
28. King James Version, Genesis 3:17, 18, 4:1, 2
29. E.G. White. *Ministry of Healing*, p. 237.
30. King James Version, Nehemiah 9:20
31. King James Version, Isaiah 33:16
32. http://www.scienceclarified.com/Ca-Ch/Carbohydrate.html viewed 2011-2-20.
33. Glucose @3dchem.com. viewed 2011-2-20
34. Neil Nedley. *Proof Positive*, p. 186.
35. Neil Nedley. *Proof Positive*, p. 273-291
36. King James Version, Isaiah 1:18
37. http://en.wikipedia.org/wiki/Fructose#cite_note-16 - wisegeek.com-what is fructose viewed 2-27-11
38. Park, KY; Yetley AE (1993). "Intakes and food sources of fructose in the United States". *American Journal of Clinical Nutrition* 58 (5 Suppl): 737S–747S. PMID 8213605. Viewed 2-19-11
39. http://en.wikipedia.org/wiki/Fructose#cite_note-16 – viewed 2-20-11
40. *How food works.com – By Marshall Brain*
41. Severson, Kim (2010-08-24). "A School Fight Over Chocolate Milk". *The New York Times*. http://www.nytimes.com/2010/08/25/dining/25Milk.html.
42. http://www.americanpregnancy.org/firstyearoflife/whatsinbreastmilk.html viewed 2-20-11
43. http://www.milkfacts.info/Milk%20Composition/protein.htm 2-21-11
44. Pamplona-Roger, G. *Foods that Heal*, p. 266.
45. King James Version, Deuteronomy 24:6
46. King James Version, 1 Kings 19:1-7
47. Common Sense Health, List of Whole Foods and Whole Grains Benefits, 2004 update, http://commonsensehealth.com/Diet-and-Nutrition/List_of_Whole_Grain_Foods_and_Whole_Grains_Benefits.shtml viewed 2-21-11
48. What Are The Dangers Of Constipation? By Yuri Elkaim, BPHE, CK, RHN & Amy Coates, RHN, BSc. http://www.totalwellnesscleanse.com/what-are-the-dangers-of-constipation.html
49. Whitney, Ellie & Rolfes, Sharon R. *Understanding Nutrition*, 10th Edition, Fiber Chart, p. 125
50. Home Cook'n Recipes for a stronger family –Kitchen Remedy Grain Cooking Chart http://www.dvo.com/newsletter/monthly/2004/february/0204remedy.html viewed 2-21-11
51. E. G. White. *Counsels on Diet & Foods*, p. 112.
52. E. G. White. *Counsels to the Church*, p. 224.
53. Ibid.
54. E. G. White. *Counsels on Diet & Foods*, p. 112.
55. Pamplona-Roger, G. *Foods that Heal*, Volume 1, p. 98.
56. E. G. White. *Counsels on Diet & Foods*, p. 112.
57. E. G. White. *Counsels on Diet & Foods*, p. 180.
58. Food Combining for Better Digestion, Article *by Jo Jordan – www.puristat.com*
59. Ibid. Emphasis added.
60. Pamplona-Roger, G. *Foods that Heal*, Volume 1, p. 98.

61. E. G. White. *Counsels on Diet & Foods*, p. 180.
62. Ibid.
63. E. G. White. *Counsels to the Church*, p. 224.
64. E. G. White. *Child Guidance*, p. 389.
65. E. G. White. *Child Guidance*, p. 64.
66. E. G. White. *Counsels on Diet & Foods*, p. 182.
67. E. G. White. *Counsels for the Church,* p. 224.
68. Ibid.
69. Ibid.
70. E. G. White. *Counsels on Diet & Foods*, #731
71. King James Version, Proverbs 24:13
72. http://www.reachoutmichigan.org/funexperiments/agesubject/lessons/tastebud.html – Taste Buds viewed 3-1-11
73. E. G. White. *Counsels for the Church*, p. 226.
74. King James Version, Proverbs 25:16, 2

THE ORIGINAL DIET
1. E. G. White. *Counsels to the Church*, p. 228.
2. E. G. White. *Counsels on Diet & Foods*, p. 373.
3. E. G. White. *Child Guidance,* p. 382.
4. Ibid.
5. E. G. White. *Counsels to the Church*, p. 228, 229.
6. E. G. White. *Counsels on Diet & Foods*, p. 375.
7. Pamplona-Roger, G. *Foods that Heal*, Magabook Version, p. 43.
8. Neil Nedley. *Proof Positive*, p. 276.
9. E. G. White. *Counsels on Diet & Foods*, p. 396.
10. Ibid, p. 375.
11. Paulien, G. B. *Divine Prescription*, pp. 219, 220.
12. Ibid.
13. E. G. White. *Counsels on Diet & Foods*, pp. 385-387.
14. Pamplona-Roger, G. *Foods that Heal,* p. 41
15. Ibid.
16. Lee, Deborah. *Essential Fatty Acids,* pp. 5-7.
17. Whitney, Ellie & Rolfes, Sharon R. *Understanding Nutrition*, 10th Edition, pp. 128, 129.
18. Balch, P. A. & Balch, J. F. *Prescription for Dietary Wellness*, p. 73.
19. Neil Nedley. *Proof Positive*, pp.73-75.
20. Pamplona-Roger, G. *Foods that Heal,* pp. 38, 39

PROTEIN
1. Whitney, Ellie & Rolfes, Sharon R. *Understanding Nutrition*, 10th Edition, p. 181
2. http://www.medicalnewstoday.com/articles/13903.php   viewed on 2-2-11
3. Pamplona-Roger, G. *Foods that Heal* p. 80.
4. King James Version, Genesis 2:9
5. King James Version, Luke 12:27
6. E. G. White. *Steps to Christ*, pp. 68, 69.
7. E. G. White. *Patriarchs and Prophets*, p. 115, 116.
8. E. G. White. *Ministry of Healing*, pp. 313, 314.
9. http://new-fitness.com/nutrition/protein.html – New Fitness – Protein viewed 2-2-11
10. E. G. White. *Ministry of Healing*, p. 316.
11. Vegetarians in Paradise, protein basics: where do you get your protein? http://www.vegparadise.com/protein.html Viewed on February 2, 2011.
12. http://www.had2know.com/culinary/conventional-oven-convection-conversion-calculator.php viewed 2-8-11
13. http://en.wikipedia.org/wiki/Food viewed 10-25-11
14. Counsels on Health, p. 450, 451. By Ellen G. White
15. Medical Ministry, p. 270. By Ellen G. White
16. Letter 279, 1905. By Ellen G. White
17. Child Guidance p. 373 By Ellen G. White
18. Ibid p. 374
19. Counsels to the Church 225 By Ellen G. White
20. Ibid p. 225
21. Child Guidance p. 374 By Ellen G. White
22. Ibid p. 376
23. Ibid p. 373
24. Counsels on Diet and Foods p. 210 – 212 By Ellen G. White
25. Ibid p. 460
26. Ministry of Healing 295 By Ellen G. White
27. Counsels to the Church p. 228 By Ellen G. White

FATS
1. http://en.wikipedia.org/wiki/Lipid viewed 3-5-11
2. http://www.scientificpsychic.com/fitness/fattyacids1.html viewed 3-5-11
3. Brown, A. *Understanding Food Principles & Preparation*, 3rd Edition.

INGREDIENTS SUBSTITUTE GUIDELINE

1. http://realfoodliving.com/faqs/sweeteners-faqs
2. Principles & Preparations Third Edition by Amy Brown
3. http://www.livestrong.com/article/8788-need-sugar-alternatives/
4. http://www.ehow.com/how_2268348_substitute-stevia-sugar-baking.html
5. http://www.madhavasweeteners.com/agave/SugarToAgaveConversion.aspx
6. Pamplona-Roger, G. *Foods that Heal,,* p. 344.
7. http://www.healthfree.com/celtic_sea_salt.html#p3
8. http://www.formerfatguyblog.com/2007/09/29/what-is-braggs-liquid-aminos.html
9. http://ths.gardenweb.com/forums/load/cooking/msg111405479224.html
10. http://www.gourmetsleuth.com/Dictionary/X/Xanthan-Gum-5756.aspx
11. http://www.barryfarm.com/nutri_info/thickeners/agar.htm
12. **http://www.gourmetsleuth.com/Dictionary/C/Carob-powder-5812.aspx**

HARMFUL BEVERAGES

1. Pamplona-Roger, G. *Foods that Heal,* p. 370.
2. Greden, J. F. et al. Anxiety and Depression Associated with Caffeinism. Veiwed 3-13-11
3. Among Psychiatric Inpatients. American Journal of Psychiatry 133:8, Aug 1978. Bellet, Samuel. Effects of Coffee Ingestion on Catecholamine Release.
4. Pamplona-Roger, G. *Foods that Heal,* p. 373.
5. Ibid.
6. Ensminger, A. H. *The Concise Encyclopedia of Foods and Nutrition.* Boca Raton (Florida), CRC Press – veiwed 3-11-11
7. E. G. White. *Counsels on Diet & Food,* p. 105.
8. E. G. White. *Child Guidance,* p. 403.
9. E. G. White. *Christian Temperance & Bible Hygiene,* pp. 34, 35.
10. CPG Sec. 555.100 Alcohol; Use of Synthetic Alcohol in Foods". Fda.gov. 2009-04-27. http://www.fda.gov/ICECI/ComplianceManuals/CompliancePolicyGuidanceManual/ucm074550.htm. Retrieved 2011 - 10-3
11. http://www.elmhurst.edu/~chm/vchembook/642alcoholmet.html
12. Pamplona-Roger, G. *Foods that Heal,* p. 337.
13. Harper, Douglas. "Etymology Online". http://www.etymonline.com/index.php?term=vinegar. Viewed 3-10-11
14. King James Version, Numbers 6:3
15. The Journal of Biological Chemistry, Volume 6 - By American Society of Biological Chemists, Rockefeller Institute for Medical Research, American Society ... retrieved 2011-10-3
16. Balch. P. *Prescription for Nutritional Healing,* p. 173.
17. Whitney, Ellie & Rolfes, Sharon R. *Understanding Nutrition,* 10th Edition, p. 49.
18. King James Version, Psalms 69:21
19. King James Version, Matthew 27:34
20. E. G. White. *Desire of Ages,* p. 746.
21. King James Version, Proverbs 10:26
22. http://lifestylelaboratory.com/articles/proof-positive/sugar-diabetes-story.htm veiwed 3-10-11

Made in the USA
Middletown, DE
04 May 2017